P9-DMB-749

Invitation to the Royal Wedding

To my mother, and best friend,

Irene Lloyd

with love

This is a Carlton book

Text & design © Carlton Books Limited 2011

itv NEWS © ITV News and ITV News logo are
trademarks and copyrighted. Used under licence from
ITV Studios Global Entertainment Ltd.

This edition published in 2011 by Carlton Books Limited
A division of the Carlton Publishing Group
20 Mortimer Street
London
W1T 3JW

This book is sold subject to the condition that it shall
not, by way of trade or otherwise, be lent, resold, hired
out or otherwise circulated without the publisher's prior
written consent in any form of cover or binding other
than that in which it is published and without a similar
condition including the condition, being imposed upon
the subsequent purchaser.

Printed in Italy

All rights reserved

A CIP catalogue for this book is available from the
British Library

ISBN: 978 1 84732 823 6

itv NEWS

Invitation to the Royal Wedding

CELEBRATING THE ENGAGEMENT OF HRH PRINCE WILLIAM OF WALES TO MISS CATHERINE MIDDLETON

IAN LLOYD

FOREWORD BY JULIE ETCHINGHAM

CARLTON
BOOKS

CONTENTS

Foreword
by Julie Etchingham

Everyone loves a good wedding and the marriage of HRH Prince William to Catherine Middleton on 29 April will clearly be no exception – an occasion watched by millions around the world, eager to enjoy the moment of history in the making.

For some of course, the news of William and Catherine's engagement will have mattered little – but for others it's been a compelling story of a truly modern royal romance. Many couples meet at university, but few are forced to conduct a relationship with such intense scrutiny from the media. In doing so, both Prince William and Catherine have clearly been mindful of lessons from the past.

There may have already been pages of newspaper print and photos dedicated to Catherine's fashion style, and to Prince William's decision to give his fiancée his mother's engagment ring, but what makes this couple really tick? *An Invitation to a Royal Wedding* gives us an insight into the real story of how these two young people have taken the time to learn about one another, to grow up together, before making a commitment which in their case has the added complexity of a royal marriage.

Thirty years ago, vast numbers revelled in celebrations surrounding the wedding of Prince William's parents. Now, the mood is different – it's low key – and William and Catherine appear to have been setting the pace. There've already been comparisons made with the wedding of the then Princess Elizabeth (now Her Majesty The Queen) to Prince Philip in the post-war climate of 1947, which acknowledged an era of austerity. In the midst of the 2011 preparations for their wedding, William and Catherine have given us a glimpse not only of their intentions for their big day, but also how they intend to shape their role as a royal couple.

As the historic occasion approaches, the following pages will take you back to where the story of William and Catherine all began, the ups and downs of its progress over the past eight years and consider the impact this young royal couple will ultimately have on Britain's future.

LEFT: Prince William and Kate Middleton enjoy a leisurely stroll – their next important walk will be down the aisle of Westminster Abbey in April.

Introduction

The Victorian journalist Walter Bagehot wrote, "A princely marriage is the brilliant edition of a universal fact, and, as such, it rivets mankind."

Weddings are not as universal as they were 150 years ago but the one between William Arthur Philip Louis Windsor and Catherine Elizabeth Middleton will be as brilliant as any the Victorians could have dreamed of and is set to rivet an estimated television audience of one billion.

Their marriage is in a sense our marriage. We are all invited and perhaps, in this more cynical age, not everyone will be dancing in the streets, but many of us will watch, listen, download, read or tweet wedding-related coverage on 29 April and for weeks afterwards.

Precedent and protocol guided twentieth-century royal courtship. Before marriage, the non-blue-blooded partner was rarely allowed to attend high profile family events or accompany their prince or princess to public engagements. The result was that they had no idea what they were letting themselves in for and went to the altar, as Diana Spencer memorably put it, "like a lamb to the slaughter".

The eight-year romance has given Kate time to grow acclimatized to life in what George VI called "the firm", with every word and action analysed by the media, every new fashion worn either criticized or lauded and every faux pas zoomed in on and highlighted.

This book looks at the personality of the bride and groom; how William's has been shaped by the twin influences of Charles and Diana, and how Kate grew strength from a close knit, middle-class family background in rural Berkshire.

From the beginnings of their romance at St Andrews to coping with its transition into a more public arena, *Invitation to the Royal Wedding* looks at the couple who will one day reign as King William V and Queen Catherine – a couple who are seen as the golden hope for the monarchy, capable of moving with the times, and making royalty relevant in the twenty-first century.

LEFT: Dress rehearsal – William and Kate turn on the style at a friend's wedding in 2010.

1
PRINCE WILLIAM

❧

"When I first met Kate I knew there was something very special about her. I knew there was possibly something that I wanted to explore there. We ended up being friends for a while and that just sort of was a good foundation. Because I do generally believe now that being friends with one another is a massive advantage. And it just went from there."

Prince William, November 2010

LEFT: On 16 November 2010 Prince William announced his engagement to Kate Middleton saying "We are both very, very happy"; the couple met at university and had been dating since 2003.

June 1982 proved to be an eventful month for the royal family. Pope John Paul II ended his visit to Britain by asking God to "bestow abundant blessings on Your Majesty"; US President Ronald Reagan, on an official visit to the UK, enjoyed an early morning horse ride with the Queen at Windsor; helicopter pilot Prince Andrew was safe and sound in the Falkland Islands as Argentine forces surrendered; and the Queen Mother welcomed home the *QE2* and her 629 troops on board. Meanwhile at St Mary's Hospital, Paddington, on 21 June HRH The Princess of Wales gave birth to a 7lb 1½ oz baby boy.

It was only 11 months earlier, on a baking hot July day, that an estimated 750 million people worldwide had tuned in to watch 20-year-old Lady Diana Spencer marry Charles, Prince of Wales at St Paul's Cathedral.

By the early autumn of 1981 Diana knew that she was pregnant, and would be the first Princess of Wales to have a baby in nearly 80 years. Both parents were naturally euphoric. They shared books on pregnancy and parenting, turned up at a lecture on childbirth and regularly attended breathing classes, which must have been a surreal distraction for all the other couples.

William Arthur Philip Louis was born at 9.03 pm, 16 hours after Diana had been admitted. A crowd of photographers, film crews and well-wishers built up during the day. When news of the birth broke, so did a rendition of "Rule Britannia", followed by "Nice One Charlie… let's have another one".

Two young men wearing only tea towels streaked past the Lindo Wing to cheers, and at the Palace Theatre, Princess Margaret received "a rapturous ovation" as dancer Wayne Sleep relayed the good news to the audience.

A letter written by the proud father a few days later to Countess Mountbatten of Burma, suggests that Charles was still mesmerized by the whole experience. "The arrival of our small son has been an astonishing experience and one that has meant more to me than I ever could have imagined…. I am so thankful I was beside Diana's bedside the whole time because by the end of the day I really felt as though I'd shared deeply in the process of birth and as a result was rewarded by seeing a small creature which belonged to us even though he seemed to belong to everyone else as well!"

ABOVE: The Prince and Princess of Wales leave St Mary's Hospital, Paddington, on 22 June 1982 with their newborn son, William; the new prince is second in line to the throne after his father.

OPPOSITE: The Queen Mother proudly holds Prince William at his christening in Buckingham Palace on 4 August 1982, flanked by The Queen and the Prince of Wales; the day also marked William's great-grandmother's 82nd birthday.

FAMILY TREE

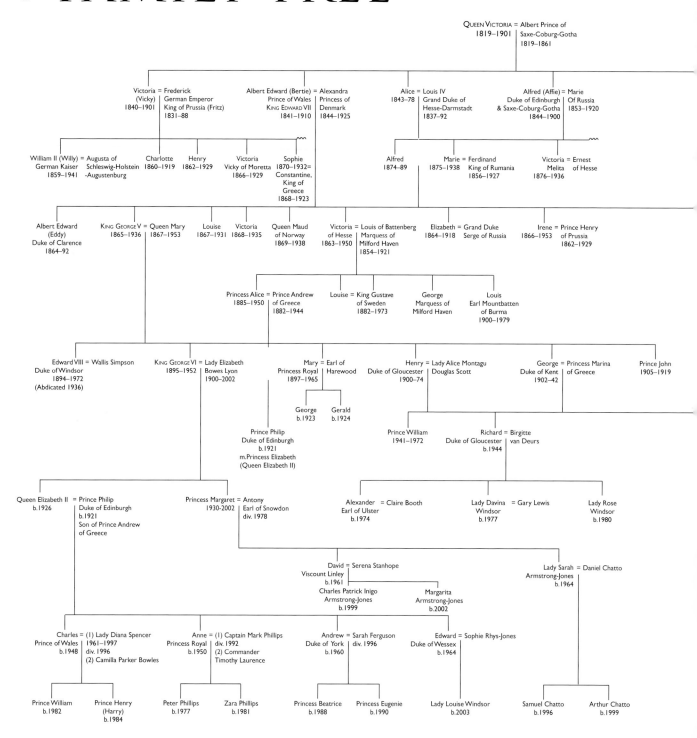

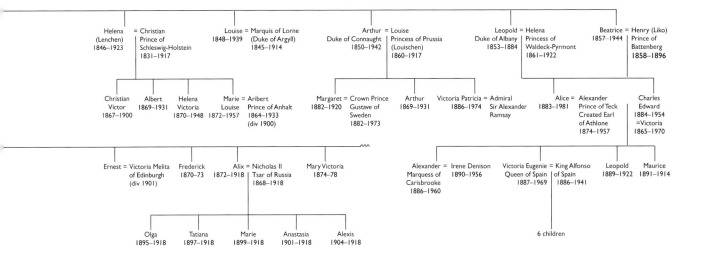

Helena (Lenchen) 1846–1923 = Christian Prince of Schleswig-Holstein 1831–1917

Louise 1848–1939 = Marquis of Lorne (Duke of Argyll) 1845–1914

Arthur Duke of Connaught 1850–1942 = Louise Princess of Prussia (Louischen) 1860–1917

Leopold Duke of Albany 1853–1884 = Helena Princess of Waldeck-Pyrmont 1861–1922

Beatrice 1857–1944 = Henry (Liko) Prince of Battenberg 1858–1896

Christian Victor 1867–1900

Albert 1869–1931

Helena Victoria 1870–1948

Marie Louise 1872–1957 = Aribert Prince of Anhalt 1864–1933 (div 1900)

Margaret 1882–1920 = Crown Prince Gustave of Sweden 1882–1973

Arthur 1869–1931

Victoria Patricia 1886–1974 = Admiral Sir Alexander Ramsay

Alice 1883–1981 = Alexander Prince of Teck Created Earl of Athlone 1874–1957

Charles Edward 1884–1954 = Victoria 1865–1970

Ernest 1870–1931 = Victoria Melita of Edinburgh (div 1901)

Frederick 1870–73

Alix 1872–1918 = Nicholas II Tsar of Russia 1868–1918

Mary Victoria 1874–78

Alexander Marquess of Carisbrooke 1886–1960 = Irene Denison 1890–1956

Victoria Eugenie Queen of Spain 1887–1969 = King Alfonso of Spain 1886–1941

Leopold 1889–1922

Maurice 1891–1914

Olga 1895–1918

Tatiana 1897–1918

Marie 1899–1918

Anastasia 1901–1918

Alexis 1904–1918

6 children

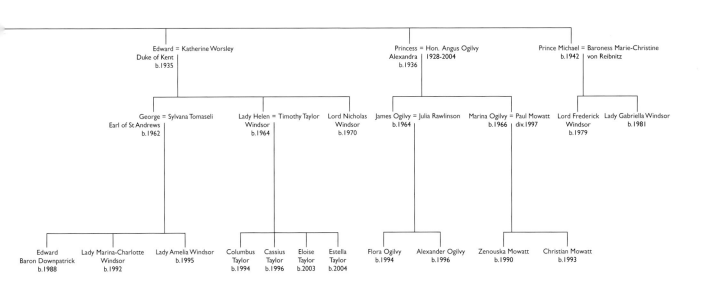

Edward Duke of Kent b.1935 = Katherine Worsley

Princess Alexandra b.1936 = Hon. Angus Ogilvy 1928-2004

Prince Michael b.1942 = Baroness Marie-Christine von Reibnitz

George Earl of St Andrews b.1962 = Sylvana Tomaseli

Lady Helen Windsor b.1964 = Timothy Taylor

Lord Nicholas Windsor b.1970

James Ogilvy b.1964 = Julia Rawlinson

Marina Ogilvy b.1966 = Paul Mowatt div.1997

Lord Frederick Windsor b.1979

Lady Gabriella Windsor b.1981

Edward Baron Downpatrick b.1988

Lady Marina-Charlotte Windsor b.1992

Lady Amelia Windsor b.1995

Columbus Taylor b.1994

Cassius Taylor b.1996

Eloise Taylor b.2003

Estella Taylor b.2004

Flora Ogilvy b.1994

Alexander Ogilvy b.1996

Zenouska Mowatt b.1990

Christian Mowatt b.1993

15

ABOVE: A joyous family scene as the proud parents play with William. Both Charles and Diana remarked on being captivated by the new arrival – the young prince, meanwhile, is captivated with the toy rattle.

The fact that the "small creature" was public property was emphasized by the media in the aftermath of his birth. "The birth of an heir is a national landmark," announced *The Times*, adding, "it is a constitutional as well as a joyous, private occasion." Like the rest of us, the new arrival could trace his ancestry back to Adam or the apes depending on your point of view, but this VIP baby could also boast 27 lines of descent from Mary, Queen of Scots, was 40th in direct line from Alfred the Great, as well as being related to Genghis Khan, Charlemagne, Rodrigo the Cid and George Washington.

Home for the newborn prince was an L-shaped apartment in Kensington Palace, newly renovated by South African designer Dudley Poplak. The nursery on the top floor comprised three bedrooms, a playroom, a kitchen and a dining room, and would be William's home for the ensuing 15 years.

With Charles and Diana in constant demand to carry out royal engagements, the baby prince spent most of his day with his nanny, Barbara Barnes, the 42-year-old daughter of a forestry worker who liked her little charges to call her by her first name and who didn't wear the formidable nursery uniforms that would have been a requirement a generation earlier.

ABOVE: The Prince and Princess of Wales manage to grab some rare family time with William in Eden Park, Auckland, during a hectic tour of Australia and New Zealand in spring 1983.

William was only nine months old when, accompanied by Nanny Barnes, he joined his parents for their six-week tour of Australia and New Zealand, clocking up more than 30,000 miles of travel. "We didn't see much of him," recalled Diana later, "but at least we were under the same sky so to speak."

On her return, Diana wrote to Maudie Pendry, her father's former housekeeper: "William has brought us such happiness and contentment and consequently I can't wait to have masses more."

Prince Harry was born on 15 September 1984 when William was just two. Any fear of sibling rivalry was quickly dispelled as Diana noted to a friend, "William adores his little brother and spends the entire time pouring an endless supply of hugs and kisses on Harry, and we are hardly allowed near."

Unfortunately the angelic phase was short lasting. By the time he was four William was creating havoc, once trying to flush his father's shoe down the lavatory and another time setting off the alarms on the Queen's Balmoral estate, resulting in police cars hurtling in from Aberdeen to seal off the grounds.

"William is getting to be quite a handful," Diana revealed to another mother on a walkabout. The press labelled him "Basher Billy" after he pushed a little girl to the ground at the Guards

ABOVE: Three-year-old Prince William sets off for his first day at nursery school, complete with a small flask of orange juice.

Polo Club, earning him a very public smacked bottom from his mother.

In September 1985, aged three he was sent to Mrs Mynors' Nursery School in Notting Hill Gate where he joined Cygnet Class which consisted of 12 pupils and one detective. His final report card, now in the Royal Archives, tells us that "Prince William was very popular with the other children, and was known for his kindness, sense of fun, and quality of thoughtfulness".

After 15 months, the prince moved on to nearby Wetherby School, where he would stay for the next three years. He was noted for his flair in English and spelling and proved he had inherited his mother's love of swimming by winning the Grunfield Cup for the best overall swimming style.

More sporting success followed at Ludgrove Preparatory School in Berkshire where he studied for five years. William was captain of the hockey and football teams and represented the school in cross-country running. It was while he was at Ludgrove that his parents announced their separation in December 1992.

The marriage of Charles and Diana had deteriorated steadily during the second half of the 1980s. During one six-week period, the couple spent only one day together, although Buckingham Palace consistently denied rumours of a rift.

Wendy Barry, the housekeeper at Highgrove, later recalled, "William was by now old enough to be aware of the rows and tensions in his parents' marriage. No amount of play-acting can ever fool a child."

Harry had joined his elder brother as a pupil at Ludgrove in September 1992. Staff were briefed to hide tabloid newspapers which were obsessively covering every twist and turn in the so-called "War of the Waleses".

The week before the announcement, Diana drove to Ludgrove to break the news of the separation to her sons. William, although only ten, took the news stoically and said, "I hope you will both be happy now." Diana later reflected on her concerns for her eldest son: "He's a child that's a deep thinker and we won't know for a few years how it has gone in. But I put it gently without any resentment or anger."

Under the terms of the separation the two princes would now divide their weekends away between Diana at Kensington Palace

ABOVE: Grandmother's wisdom: Prince Harry and Prince William are given some tips on polo from the Queen at the Guards Polo Club, Windsor, in June 1987. Both boys would later take up the sport.

and Charles at Highgrove House in Gloucestershire.

Diana was keen that William should respect his royal heritage. Initially, she maintained a warm association with her former mother-in-law, telling one friend, "It's very important to me that my sons have a very good relationship with the Queen." She also hated criticism of Charles by third parties: "The princess never liked that sort of thing and would rebuke them saying, 'Remember that he's the father of my children,'" recalled her friend Roberto Devorik, the fashion entrepreneur.

Weekends with the princess often involved treats – from burgers at McDonalds in Kensington High Street to white-knuckle rides at Alton Towers in Staffordshire. There were also visits to Disney World in Florida, holidays in the Caribbean and white water rafting in Colorado.

At Highgrove, William grew accustomed to country pursuits from an early age. The 348 acres of parkland were perfect for bike rides, skateboarding and riding his Shetland pony away

from the prying eyes of the public. Later he enjoyed shooting and stalking with his father on the Queen's estates, as well as polo – Charles bought him a polo pony for his 17th birthday.

The family would put on a united front at occasional royal engagements, such as the anniversaries of VE Day and VJ Day in the summer of 1995. Also that September, Charles and Diana posed for photos with their two sons when William arrived to study at Eton College.

In July 1997 a helicopter landed in the grounds of Kensington Palace to take Diana, William and Harry on what would turn out to be their final holiday together. Mohamed Al Fayed, the Egyptian-born owner of Harrods International, had invited them to stay on his yacht *Jonikal* which then headed for St Tropez where the family owned a villa.

It was during this cruise that Diana was introduced to Al Fayed's 42-year-old son, Dodi. The two began a highly publicized affair that tragically ended with their deaths in an horrific car crash in Paris just six weeks later.

The young princes were staying at Balmoral Castle with

ABOVE: Princess Diana and her two princes enjoy a splash on a water ride at the Thorpe Park amusement park in April 1993.

OPPOSITE: The Prince and Princess of Wales pose with William and Harry on the steps of the Spanish royal residence Marivent Palace on the island of Majorca during a family holiday in August 1987.

their father when Diana died. Both Charles and the Queen were woken in the early hours of the morning when news of the accident was forwarded from Buckingham Palace. The prince decided to let his sons sleep on until 7.30 when they normally awoke. Fifteen minutes later he went to their adjoining rooms to break the news to them that their mother was dead.

During the days that followed William and Harry showed remarkable self-control and maturity beyond their years; indeed, they faced the cameras less than four hours after hearing the news when they attended a church service at Crathie Kirk.

Later in the week they again remained composed when they took flowers from well-wishers in the grounds of Kensington Palace, while across London their grandmother paid a television tribute to Diana praising "her energy and commitment to others, especially her two boys".

The following day the two princes stood shoulder to shoulder with their father, their grandfather Prince Philip, and their uncle Earl Spencer as Diana's cortège slowly moved into view along the Mall. Under the gaze of thousands of onlookers and millions of television viewers, the boys walked behind their mother's coffin as it made its farewell journey through the capital.

ABOVE: The Queen and Prince William, pictured on the Buckingham Palace balcony with Princess Margaret and Prince Philip, acknowledge the crowd during June 1990's Trooping the Colour parade.

Diana once said that William and Harry were the only two men who had never let her down and in the years that followed they have continued to protect her memory and her legacy. During these years everyone –from lovers and "friends" to therapists and hairdressers – has cashed in on the very lucrative market for Diana-related memoirs. William has publicly condemned many of them and, aged only 16, asked for a statement to be made on the first anniversary of his mother's death, in which he and his brother thanked people for mourning his mother but suggested it was time to move on and to look forwards rather than backwards.

Charles now reconstructed his work and leisure time so that his world could revolve around his two young sons. After their first Christmas without their mother, he took them to Klosters for a week's skiing. On their return, he announced that he would be "streamlining" his charities in order to spend more time with them. The boys joined him in March 1998 for a visit to British Columbia in Canada during which William was given a rapturous welcome from thousands of Vancouver's teenagers.

In another sensitive gesture Charles asked interior designer Robert Kime to recreate the boys' Kensington Palace suite of rooms as closely as possible in an apartment at St James's Palace.

In June of 1998, nine days before his 16th birthday, William was finally introduced to Camilla Parker Bowles at St James's. The two had what was later called "a cordial and general discussion about all manner of things." The two met again for

LEFT: Prince Harry shares a comment with his elder brother, much to their mother's amusement. Along with Princes Charles, they were attending the VJ Day commemorations staged outside Buckingham Palace in August 1995. The event, which marked the 60th anniversary of victory over Japan in the Second World War, was attended by 15,000 veterans and tens of thousands of spectators

tea shortly afterwards and by the end of the year were jointly planning Charles's 50th birthday party at Highgrove in which William and Harry starred in a comedy play produced by Oscar-winning actress Emma Thompson and Stephen Fry.

In the summer of 1998 William passed nine GCSEs with A grades in English, History and Languages. He had already passed three others the previous year, and the royal family was said to be "privately delighted" that William had been so successful despite the trauma of his mother's death.

In his final two years at Eton, William won the Sword of Honour as best cadet in the Eton College Officer Training Corps. He was also elected a member of Pop, the college's élite group of 19 prefects responsible for supervising the other 1,260 boys.

The prince's A Level passes – an A grade in Geography, a B in History and a C in Biology – confirmed his status as one of the brightest royals. It also meant that he gained his university place at St Andrews on merit rather than favouritism.

Charles was keen that his son should take a year off before continuing his academic career so that he could see

ABOVE: Prince William signs the register at Eton College in 1995 watched by his parents and younger brother; this is when we learned that William was left-handed.

OPPOSITE ABOVE: William's confirmation took place at St George's Chapel in March 1997 – this was the last time Diana was present at a royal event. Here, they pose in the White Drawing Room at Windsor Castle with his five surviving godparents, ex-King Constantine of Greece, Lady Susan Hussey, Princess Alexandra, the Duchess of Westminster and Lord Romsey. The sixth godparent Sir Laurent van der Post had died the previous year.

OPPOSITE BELOW: Soldiers of the 1st Battalion, Welsh Guards carry Diana's coffin into Westminster Abbey for her funeral on 6 September 1997. Behind it walk Prince Charles, Prince Harry, Earl Spencer, Prince William and Prince Philip.

something of the world and take advantage of the fact that the media was so far respecting his privacy.

He opted to join 15 other volunteers for a ten-week Raleigh International project in the remote community of Tortel, deep in the heart of the Andes. Here, he slept on the floor, cleaned the toilets, chopped firewood and made some "absolutely foul" porridge. TV coverage of the visit gave a glimpse of his natural affinity with children when he acted as a classroom assistant in a nursery school, and his six-year-old charges in turn leaped on his back and insisted he carry them around.

During his year off William also joined his father's regiment, the Welsh Guards, to take part in training exercises in the jungles of Belize. Then in September 2000 he headed for Mauritius to carry out an educational programme with the Royal Geographical Society.

Ironically, given the vast amount of travel and the exotic locations, William's favourite part of his year off was the short time he spent much closer to home. "The best bit was in

ABOVE: On a March 1998 visit to Vancouver, Canada, with his father and brother, William shows his impish side – having been presented with Canadian Olympic jackets and baseball caps, William decides to put his hat on back to front.

LEFT: William arrives at Highgrove House, the Gloucestershire country home of the Prince of Wales, in summer 1999 after a driving lesson. William had been driving on the private roads of the Royal estates from the age of 13, but received just 20 hours of tuition from Police Sergeant Chris Gilbert, an expert in anti-hijack and counter-surveillance techniques, before passing his driving test in a silver Ford Focus

England," he told a journalist before starting at university. "I loved working on a farm, before foot and mouth, which is why I've got so much sympathy for the farmers who have suffered so much from it. It was the best part of my year. I got my hands dirty, did all the chores, and had to get up 4.00 am. I got to see a completely different lifestyle."

Having stretched himself physically it was now time for William to resume his academic career. Aged 19, he said that he had little idea what the next four years would hold; he couldn't know that he was about to meet the woman who would one day become his wife.

2
CATHERINE MIDDLETON

"Kate had a certain presence. She was a very mature girl. She was a very attractive girl, she was a very popular girl, particularly popular with the boys, and she was a great member of the expedition. But she was always very in control of herself and impeccably behaved."

Rachel Humphrey, who looked after Kate and other volunteers on a project in Chile in 2001

LEFT: On her first official appearance after their engagement was announced, Kate Middleton joined her husband-to-be at a charity event in Norfolk in December 2010 – all a far cry from the initial camaraderie that developed during their early days at university.

ABOVE: Prince William's future fiancée lived in the Berkshire village of Bradfield Southend – about seven miles from Reading – until she was 13. It was while the family lived here that Carole Middleton began the business that became Party Pieces, enabling them to move to a bigger property.

The moment a royal engagement is announced, genealogists always scour their archives in an attempt to find a familial link between the two parties.

The results are often fascinating. Prince William's mother Diana, his stepmother Camilla and his former aunt Sarah, Duchess of York, are all descended from Charles II through some of his many illegitimate sons.

Diana was related to Winston Churchill as well as eight US presidents including Franklin Roosevelt and George W. Bush. Through her mother, Camilla is descended from one Zacharie Cloutier, a French carpenter who emigrated to Canada in the early sixtenth century. This makes her a distant relation of his other descendants, such as Hillary Clinton, Celine Dion, Angelina Jolie, Jack Kerouac and Madonna.

Kate's solidly middle-class background wouldn't automatically promise rich pickings for the researchers at the National Archives, but the more tenacious ones did find a link with Prince William. He and Kate are, it seems, related to Sir Thomas Leighton, an Elizabethan soldier, diplomat and for 40 years the Governor of Guernsey. He is the prince's 12th generation great-grandparent and Kate's 11th, making them 12th cousins once removed.

Leighton had a reputation as a despot and dictator. One of the accounts of his life says, "He disregarded civil liberties and kept the people down by main force." He was fond of imprisonment without trial, and press-ganged Guernseymen to go to sea to fight pirates.

Queen Elizabeth I turned a blind eye to his failings and was thankful that he effectively defended this vulnerable part of her realm from the continuing threat of a Spanish invasion. As a reward she offered him a knighthood and the hand of her cousin Elizabeth Knollys in marriage. The latter was a great-niece of the queen's mother, Anne Boleyn, to whom it's been suggested Kate bears more than a passing resemblance.

Kate and William are also both descended from King Edward III, famed for his crushing victory over the French at the Battle of Crécy in 1346.

Among Kate's other antecedents are Harriet Martineau, often cited as the first woman sociologist and the author of academic

ABOVE: From Bradfield Southend the Middletons moved the short distance to Bucklebury. In recent times the royal connection has led to uniformed firearms officers brandishing semi-automatic machine guns patrolling the grounds.

treatises such as *How to Observe Morals and Manners*. She also wrote allegorical novels including, to the delight of the researchers, *The Peasant and the Prince*.

Finally there are vague connections between other writers and Kate's family. She is a distant cousin of the children's author Beatrix Potter, and is also related to Arthur Ransome, who produced *Swallows and Amazons*. Ransome's sister Joyce was married to Hugo Lupton, the cousin of Kate's great-grandmother Olive.

The Luptons, Kate's ancestors on her father's side, were comfortably-off stalwarts of Leeds society in the late nineteenth and early twentieth centuries. Olive was the daughter of Francis Martineau Lupton, a former member of Leeds City Council, whose life was blighted by tragedy – his wife died at the age of 42 and all three of their sons were killed in the First World War. Olive married Noel Middleton, who worked as a solicitor and whose father was president of Leeds Law Society and the founder of the Leeds and County Conservative Club.

On her mother's side Kate's ancestors were of solid working-class stock. Take for instance James Harrison, who started work

FAMILY TREE

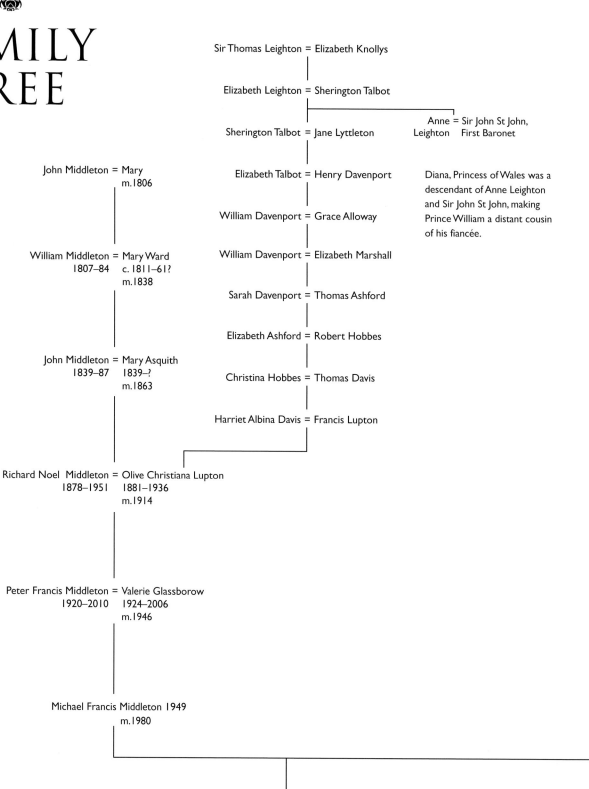

Sir Thomas Leighton = Elizabeth Knollys

Elizabeth Leighton = Sherington Talbot

Sherington Talbot = Jane Lyttleton

Anne = Sir John St John,
Leighton   First Baronet

John Middleton = Mary
m.1806

Elizabeth Talbot = Henry Davenport

Diana, Princess of Wales was a
descendant of Anne Leighton
and Sir John St John, making
Prince William a distant cousin
of his fiancée.

William Davenport = Grace Alloway

William Middleton = Mary Ward
1807–84   c.1811–61?
m.1838

William Davenport = Elizabeth Marshall

Sarah Davenport = Thomas Ashford

Elizabeth Ashford = Robert Hobbes

John Middleton = Mary Asquith
1839–87   1839–?
m.1863

Christina Hobbes = Thomas Davis

Harriet Albina Davis = Francis Lupton

Richard Noel Middleton = Olive Christiana Lupton
1878–1951   1881–1936
m.1914

Peter Francis Middleton = Valerie Glassborow
1920–2010   1924–2006
m.1946

Michael Francis Middleton 1949
m.1980

Catherine Middleton 1982

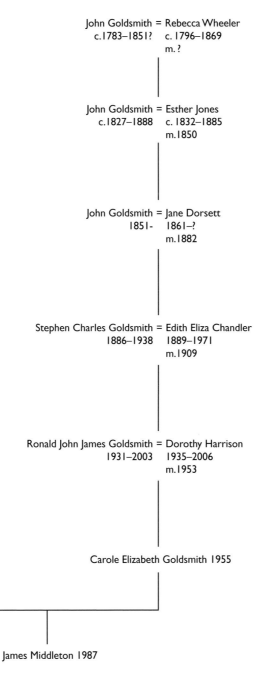

John Goldsmith = Rebecca Wheeler
c.1783–1851? c.1796–1869
m. ?

John Goldsmith = Esther Jones
c.1827–1888 c.1832–1885
m.1850

John Goldsmith = Jane Dorsett
1851- 1861–?
m.1882

Stephen Charles Goldsmith = Edith Eliza Chandler
1886–1938 1889–1971
m.1909

Ronald John James Goldsmith = Dorothy Harrison
1931–2003 1935–2006
m.1953

Carole Elizabeth Goldsmith 1955

Pippa Middleton 1983   James Middleton 1987

ABOVE: During her time at St Andrew's School in Pangbourne, Berkshire, Kate excelled at a number of sports including tennis, swimming, netball, hockey and rounders. Kate, pictured in the middle of the front row, was the highest scorer on the under-12/13 rounders team.

as a miner in the coalfields of County Durham in 1819, the year of Queen Victoria's birth. Generations of the family would work in the same profession. When they weren't facing daily threats to their lives below ground – there were 30 major disasters in the Durham area between 1800 and 1899 – above ground the Harrisons fell pray to cholera, typhoid and the other diseases that were rife in the poorly sanitized slums of Victorian England.

The fortunes of Kate's family were to change again radically as recently as the 1980s thanks to the hard work of her parents. Michael Middleton is seven months younger than Prince Charles; Kate's mother Carole, born in 1955, is six years younger than her husband.

The couple had met in the 1970s when they both worked for British Airways (BA). Carole Goldsmith was an air stewardess and Michael was a flight dispatcher. His father Peter had been a pilot instructor, but Michael himself switched from pilot training to ground crew. His job was to co-ordinate the aircraft between arrival and departure – which involved everything from

ABOVE RIGHT: Kate celebrates another hockey victory; her sporting prowess at St Andrew's was such that on prize-giving day she was awarded a cup for outstanding sporting achievement.

monitoring fuel intake to authorising take-off. He was the same grade as a captain and wore a similar uniform.

Carole was glamorous and a good catch for Michael who became her first serious boyfriend. He was quiet and unassuming and, as we have seen, could trace his family back to nobility through his grandmother Olive.

After dating for several years, the couple set up home in the Berkshire village of Bradfield Southend, some seven miles west of Reading. They married eight months later in June 1980 in the village of Dorney, with the 25-year-old bride arriving by horse and carriage.

Catherine Elizabeth Middleton was born on 9 January 1982 at the Royal Berkshire Hospital at Reading, coming into the world more than five months ahead of her future husband.

She was christened at the fourteenth-century church of St Andrew's, near to the River Pang, and wore a traditional white gown. Afterwards, the family celebrated at the local manor.

Her younger sister Philippa, known as Pippa, was born at the same hospital 20 months later on 6 September 1985, and their only brother, James William, was born in April 1987 when Kate was five.

For the first 13 years of Kate's life the family lived in the village of Bradfield Southend. This is less than a ten-minute drive to where the Middletons live now, so while Prince William divided his time between Highgrove in Gloucestershire, Kensington Palace in London and assorted royal estates in England and Scotland, Kate's home life for nearly 30 years has centred around the same four-mile area of Berkshire.

Young Kate and Pippa were taken by their mother to the toddlers' playgroup held at St Peter's Church Hall on Tuesday mornings. Later on, the girls would walk to the same building when they became Brownies in the 1st St Andrew's pack of 24. As toddlers, they also joined other village children at St Peter's Preschool run by the wife of the churchwarden.

At the age of four Kate started at the local school, Bradfield Church of England Primary School, which was conveniently

OPPOSITE: At the end of her time at St Andrew's prep school, Kate presented this Picasso print to her house "parents", Kevin and Denise Allford, complete with a handwritten note of thanks on the reverse. However, in trimming the print to make it fit the frame, Mrs Allford chopped part of the message, too!

BELOW: Kate, pictured on the far left of this line-up, was a popular pupil at St Andrew's. It was at St Andrew's, as a ten-year-old, that she first saw William when, amid great excitement, the nine-year-old prince came to the school to play a hockey match

situated next door to the Middletons' home. Here the future
princess showed a healthy interest in sport – enjoying rounders,
athletics and frequently swimming in the unheated outdoor pool,
which she also used during her summer holidays. It was while
she was at this school that Kate took her cycling proficiency test.
She has remained a keen cyclist ever since and was often spotted
biking to lectures at St Andrews.

Michael Middleton was still working for BA, but Carole,
with three children to look after, also found time to make party
bags which she sold to other mums while Kate was still a toddler.
This seed of an idea eventually germinated into Party Pieces
which Carole founded around the time of James's birth "to
inspire other mothers to create magical parties at home and to
make party organising a little easier".

James later recalled "great childhood memories of my mother
baking cakes and I was always willing to participate, especially
if it meant that I could lick the bowl and revarnish the floor with
treacle".

Carole hired a unit at Yattendon, four miles from her home,
to store the merchandise. She now began sending out basic
catalogues which included photos of her three children dressed in
t-shirts with their ages printed on them, and holding cup cakes.

Kate's only written interview to date appeared briefly on
the Party Pieces website in March 2010. Anyone logging on
in the hope of hearing an exposé on her royal love life was
disappointed, as her comments were confined to the party theme
and her memories are as sugary as one of Carole's cakes. She told
how she used to love dressing up as a clown in giant dungarees
and playing musical statues as a child because she has "always
been a keen dancer". Asked what she thought would make
a good party bag, she replied, "Anything that Mummy would
normally never allow me to have. They were always such
a treat."

Kate went on to describe music as a "great ice breaker for
any party" and listed her best party memory as the "amazing
white rabbit marshmallow cake that Mummy made when I was
seven". Her own venture into the kitchen was "a cake disaster"
as she forgot to add the self-raising flour and her flat sponge
ended up as the bottom half of a trifle.

In the autumn of 1989, Kate was sent to the co-educational St Andrew's School in Pangbourne, four miles from home. Again, she excelled at sport, winning swimming races and joining the netball team. She was also good at the high jump and broke the school record for her age group.

Kate was also keen on amateur theatricals, starring in the school production of the Tchaikovsky ballet *The Nutcracker* and taking the role of Eliza Doolittle in *My Fair Lady*. In her final year she starred as the heroine in a Victorian melodrama, which was videoed at the time and has since been on several TV documentaries mainly because her love interest in the play was called William. In one scene he falls to his knees and asks her to marry him. She replies, "Yes, it's all I've ever longed for. Yes, oh yes, dear William... Ah to think I am loved by such a splendid gentleman." Sadly, by the end of the play, the Pangbourne William had dumped her and her baby, and was never heard of again.

By the time Kate was a teenager, Party Pieces was flourishing. Not only did it have its own website but the name was registered with Companies House to prevent anyone else using it. Carole's company moved into a set of farm buildings in Ashampstead

PREVIOUS PAGE: Kate is pictured with one of her Marlborough College pals, Gemma Williamson. Gemma recalls Kate as a conservative dresser: "Kate never wore particularly fashionable or revealing clothes – just jeans and jumpers with discreet pearl earrings and lots of bangles."

Common and by then had expanded enough to take on a staff of eight.

In July 1995, when Kate was 13, the family moved to its present home on the outskirts of Chapel Row, in the parish of Bucklebury, a typical English village with a pub, tearooms and a village green.

The following April Kate arrived at Marlborough School, founded in 1843 in the Wiltshire town of the same name. Old Marlburians include John Betjeman, singer Chris de Burgh, Princess Anne's former husband Mark Phillips, the BBC's security correspondent Frank Gardner and, since Kate's time, Princess Eugenie.

The school had been fully co-educational for only six years, and Kate moved into the girls' boarding house, Elmhurst. What definitely appealed to her were the tremendous sports facilities – the college boasts 11 rugby pitches, seven soccer pitches, six hockey pitches and a dozen tennis courts. She eventually captained the school hockey team and would regularly play tennis.

Several friends from her Marlborough days have given newspaper interviews and none of them has a bad word to say about Kate. Kathryn Solari who studied biology with her recalls: "Catherine was always really sweet and lovely. She treated everyone alike. She was a good girl and quite preppy – she always did the right thing – and she was very, very sporty. I wouldn't say she was the brightest button but she was very hard-working."

Former classmate Charlie Leslie described Kate as "level-headed and down to earth." She said: "Kate is an absolutely phenomenal girl – really popular, talented, creative and sporty." One college master described her as an A-grade pupil and an all-rounder who was popular throughout the school.

Thankfully for Kate's present role, there seem to be few, if any skeletons in her cupboard. "I never once saw her drunk," recalls Jessica Hay. "Even after our GCSEs finished, she only drank a couple of glugs of vodka."

She was similarly abstemious when it came to romance. The only name linked to her from her schooldays is fellow student Willem Marx, whom one school chum claims was "her first

OPPOSITE: At 13, Kate went to Marlborough School; a schoolmate has since revealed that Kate kept a poster of Prince William in her dorm room and said – perhaps in jest – that she would marry him one day

41

*LEFT: It would seem that Kate's
mother has long been preparing
for a special wedding – Carole
Goldsmith, who today is the mother
of the princess-in-waiting, is pictured
here aged five as a bridesmaid
in 1960.*

love", though Marx, now a 28-year-old journalist, steadfastly refuses to talk about any relationship they may have had.

Kate passed her 11 GCSEs with flying colours. She returned the following term to begin her A level studies and friends noticed a change that summer of 1998. "She came back an absolute beauty," remembers Gemma Williamson. "She never wore particularly fashionable or revealing clothes – just jeans and a jumper – but she had an innate sense of style."

Kate's time at Marlborough paid off and in her A Levels she gained A grades in Mathematics and Art as well as a B in English.

Like William, the next stage for Kate was a year off. Two months after graduating, she stayed in Florence where she immersed herself in the city's rich legacy of paintings and

BELOW: Michael and Carole Middleton arrive at the Concert for Diana at Wembley Stadium in July 2007; Kate's parents set up a mail order firm, Party Pieces, in 1987 which, through the advent of the internet, became a huge success.

ABOVE: *Kate and her mother Carole visit the Spirit of Christmas shopping festival at London's Olympia in November 2005.*

sculptures. Arriving in September 2000, she studied Italian for 12 weeks in a class of a dozen girls at the British Institute. She shared a flat above an Italian delicatessen with a group that included singer Chris Rea's niece, Alice Whitaker.

After Florence, Kate joined Raleigh International, co-incidentally the same organization that William had joined. Like the prince, Kate went to Chile, though not on the same expedition; hers was in the spring of 2001, several months after William had returned.

Malcolm Sutherland from Ross-shire, who worked for Raleigh International at the time, met them both and recalls, "For ten weeks each lived with absolutely no luxuries. This was roughing it by anyone's standards.

"Kate's trip involved three weeks of trekking, three weeks on a marine survey and her remaining weeks on a community.

"There was absolutely no connection between the couple at

that stage and it's an incredible coincidence that they chose the same company and the same organization, but I think it shows how well suited William and Kate are."

Malcolm feels they will make a great couple: "She's an incredibly straightforward down-to-earth girl. I think she'd be supportive to William but not subservient. She's a modern girl, hugely intelligent and fun. I think she's exactly what the monarchy needs."

Kate's family tree with its emphasis on hard work, community service and moral integrity, down through the generations, has reached fruition in Kate. The confidence she gained from her close-knit family, her academic success, her love of sport and her faultless personality would all equip her to face her next stage in life – university.

RIGHT: Kate's brother and sister, James and Pippa – seen here at an Issa show during London Fashion Week in February 2010 – both followed her to Marlborough College.

3

ST ANDREWS

"Clearly this year there will be an unprecedented number of people accepting places at St Andrews. I would like to say this was down to the excellent academic standards, but it is pretty obvious much of this is to do with a new student. St Andrews has more pubs per square foot than any other town in Scotland, although the nearest nightclub is in Dundee. Every night there is something happening, lots of dinners, lots of balls. We like to work hard and play hard."

Marcus Booth, president of the students' sssociation at the University of St Andrews

LEFT: Prince William studies in the main university library at St Andrews, Fife, on the east coast of Scotland. The university, the oldest in Scotland, became especially popular when it was known that the prince had enrolled there in 2001.

"I just want to go to university and have fun," said 19-year-old Prince William as he prepared for four years of study at St Andrews, Scotland's oldest university. He added: "I want to go there and be an ordinary student. I mean I'm only going to university. It's not like I'm getting married – though that's what it feels like sometimes."

Ten years on, his words are ironic. Little did he realize back in 2001 that the path to academic success would also lead to the altar.

It had been expected that the prince would study either at

LEFT: A nervous Prince William – or William Wales as he'd be known at St Andrews – arrives for his first day at university in September 2001, with his father along for moral support.

Oxford or perhaps follow in his father's footsteps and attend Trinity College, Cambridge. In the end it was the beauty of St Andrews that caught his eye – although another major factor was that it was about as far away from prying paparazzi lenses as he could get.

William had opted for the four-year History of Art course. The fact that his granny happens to own more than 7,000 paintings by Rubens, Titian, Vermeer, Gainsborough and so on, would after all give him a bit of a head start over his classmates.

The Queen was apparently delighted with the choice of university; it was where the Scottish King James V had studied and where in 1929 her own mother was given an honorary degree.

With the approach of the start date, 23 September 2001, the prince became increasingly nervous. Prince Charles arranged to take him to college and on the way there they dropped in for lunch with the Queen Mother at Birkhall, her Deeside home.

The 101-year-old lady sensed that her great grandson was apprehensive and, kissing him a fond farewell, she joked, "Any good parties, invite me down!"

ABOVE: On his arrival at St Andrews, William was warmly greeted by an enthusiastic crowd – plus the inevitable bank of photographers.

OVERLEAF: The view over St Andrews town and the Cathedral ruins. Prince William and a certain Kate Middleton would be studying at the town's university until June 2005.

William had chosen St Salvator's Hall, or "Sallys" as he would soon call it, where he would stay for the next year in a suite of rooms large enough to accommodate his ever-present security team.

The much-publicized news of the prince's intention to study at St Andrews led to the so-called "Wills Factor" which altered the normal male–female ratio, thanks to a 44-per cent increase in applications, most of them female.

Arriving at college is nerve-wracking enough for anyone, but to pull up outside his new hall of residence in the family car with 3,000 locals and 100 photographers watching his every move must have been mortifying for William. Blushing strongly and with his hands firmly rammed into the pockets of his faded denims, William looked awkward as the fans and well-wishers cheered his arrival. Prince Charles tried his best to dress down,

ABOVE: Prince William poses in the grounds of Holyrood House, Edinburgh, the official residence of the monarch in Scotland, a couple of days before his first term at university. Behind the prince is Arthur's Seat, an extinct volcano.

OPPOSITE: Two years into his university course, William enjoys a barefoot stroll along one of Fife's sandy beaches. To allow the prince to study in peace a deal was struck with the British media who agreed to give him some space in return for occasional photocalls.

ABOVE: Overwhelmed by the whole university experience in his first year, William's interest was reignited in more ways than one when he took his front-row seat at a university charity fashion show during his second term – among the girls parading along the catwalk was a scantily-clad Kate Middleton

wearing white slacks with brown suede shoes, though his double-breasted jacket with a pink silk hankie in the top pocket put him firmly in the "embarrassing Dads" category.

To ensure that William could study in peace, a deal was struck between Prince Charles's office and the British media, whereby the press would back off in return for occasional photocalls at which the prince would also give an interview.

Within days, however, the prince's privacy was invaded when a camera crew was spotted filming in and around St Salvator's. Embarrassingly for the royal family it turned out to be a team from Ardent Productions, the company owned by Prince Edward. Ardent was making a film called an *A–Z of Royalty* for a California-based entertainment network. Prince Charles's spokeswoman announced he was "disappointed, very much so". The *A–Z* crew was unceremoniously asked to leave St Andrews, presumably without its *W for William*.

University is a great social leveller, and once he had dropped his royal title and became William Wales – or plain "Will" to his new mates – he soon melted into the background. Like the rest of the students he wore jeans, shirt and a jumper – or more often a fleece, to keep out those east-coast breezes.

The prince loved the fact that the town's 16,000 citizens let him be. He could shop in Tesco unnoticed or buy a paper in the local newsagents usually without any hassle. He later joked, "I've had a grandmother stop me and ask me if I know a good place to buy underwear!" Clearly she had no idea who it was who gave her directions to the nearest lingerie shop.

He was even able to take part in the university's traditional Raisin Monday in the November of his first year. Around a thousand students dress up in fancy dress and have shaving foam fights, and William was in the thick of it this time around, covered in foam and with his head painted blue.

To help him settle in, William made use of the student support network designed to help first-year students settle in. Older undergraduates act as "parents", passing on advice and tips on surviving what can be an ordeal to the uninitiated. St Andrews helps to create a family feeling by referring to these mentors as mothers and fathers. William's "mother" was Alice Drummond-Hay from Connecticut, USA, whose grandfather

ABOVE: Kate Middleton, a future flatmate of William but at this point dating a fourth-year student, evidently made her mark at the university fashion show of March 2002 with this daring outfit – a sheer black lace dress over a bandeau bra and black bikini bottoms

the Earl of Crawford and Balcarries, was Lord Chamberlain to the Queen Mother. His "father" was an old Etonian called Gus McMyn.

Making friends when you are a prince isn't easy, though William was confident of his ability to gauge true characters amid the many new faces at St Andrews. "People who try to take advantage of me and get a piece of me I spot it quickly and soon go off them. I'm not stupid," he said.

No doubt he was as astute when it came to meeting women. During his time at "Sallys" William kept bumping into the same attractive brunette. Kate Middleton was more shy and demure than the other girls, though, to her embarrassment, she had already been labelled the prettiest girl at "Sallys" by the end of Freshers' Week.

Not only did they share the same hall of residence but they were also on the same course, and when there was a clash of timetable, Kate would take notes for Will and vice versa.

They had a great deal in common. For a start, they both shared a love of sport. Kate would get up early and be out jogging before breakfast, often arriving back just before the canteen closed. William timed his own breakfast to coincide and invited her to join his group. The pair shared a passion for swimming and would swim together most mornings at the luxury Old Course Hotel. There were no lessons on Wednesday afternoons and the prince trained for both rugby and Sunday league football. Later on, he became an avid member of the water polo team.

St Andrews is legendary for having more pubs per square mile than any other Scottish town. William however tended to keep a low profile, admitting, "I am not a party animal." He preferred dinner parties with friends to propping up the bar, although he would occasionally go to the Bop, the weekly disco on Market Street.

At the end of his first term William had what he later referred to as "a wobble". He was feeling overwhelmed by the whole university experience and later admitted, "I don't think I was homesick; I was more daunted." His father was deeply concerned, while Prince Philip's attitude was typically more robust and he told his grandson just to "get on with it". Had

William left it would have been a PR disaster for the monarchy, particularly in Scotland, and on a more personal level it would have made William appear to be a "quitter", a label that haunted Prince Edward for years after he walked out on his training with the marines after only four months.

Although he and Kate were good friends, it was just a platonic relationship at the time, since Kate was dating Rupert Finch, a fourth-year student. However it was Kate who persuaded him to change his course to Geography and he felt relieved and happy with the switch.

It was during his second term that cupid's dart hit William one evening at the end of March 2002. It was the night of the annual Don't Walk charity fashion show at the five-star St Andrews Bay Hotel.

The prince had paid £200 for his front-row seat and his eyes nearly popped out of his head when Kate walked down the catwalk wearing a see-through dress and black underwear.

Afterwards, there was a party at 14 Hope Street, a student house, and William made his move, engaging Kate in a long conversation and leaning in for a kiss. Kate who was still dating Rupert, rebuffed him.

William had to bide his time and, for the time being, they remained just good friends. This was still the case in September of that year when Kate, Fergus Boyd and Olivia Bleasdale moved into a shared flat with the prince at 13a Hope Street. The four of them paid £100 a week rent and shared the cooking and cleaning.

When it was his turn to cook, William did all his own shopping and managed a few tried and trusted recipes as he recalled later on when he was asked about his kitchen skills: "I've done a bit at university when I had to feed my flatmates, which was quite hard work as a couple of them ate quite a lot."

At some point in the next few months Kate and William became a couple, though they went to elaborate lengths to hide it, arriving and leaving the flat and lecture halls separately, and never holding hands or going to parties together.

Jules Knight, part of the classical vocal quartet Blake, was a guest at some of William and Kate's parties at Hope Street. He recalls a legendary evening when someone set off the fire alarm.

ABOVE: Graduation day delight! Kate's four-year university course culminated with a 2:1 degree in Art History and she and William both graduated on 23 June 2005.

OPPOSITE: By August 2004 when Kate posed for this fashion shot at the Game Fair at Blenheim Palace, she and William were an item – although the pair took great pains to hide the fact.

"Will climbed on to a door handle and then on to the door to turn off the fuse box. Of course it also turned off the security system and the next thing security officers burst in with guns at the ready."

Although the couple were happy to stay in watching DVDs or ordering takeaways, they would go out with friends to the West Port bar on South Street or to Ma Bells, where many students met, beneath the Golf Hotel on the Scores. Then there was the Lizard on North Street, where they could enjoy a late night dance or two.

ABOVE: The Queen and Prince Philip join the newly wed Duke and Duchess of Rothesay for Prince William's graduation ceremony at St Andrews in June 2005.

RIGHT: Having attained a class 2:1 degree in Geography, Prince William leaves St Andrews in his graduation robe. Well-wishers lined the streets and the prince made a point of thanking them for helping to make his stay so enjoyable.

FAVOURITE HAUNTS: Among Kate and William's favourite places in St Andrews were: (left) Sophie Butler Hairdressing, where Kate would have her hair done; the Anstruther Fish Bar (bottom left), whose award-winning fish and chips were much admired by William; the Gin House, nowadays called The Rule (top right), and Ma Bells (bottom right) where the couple would enjoy a drink or two with their friends.

At the start of their third year, William and Kate moved to Balgove House on the Strathtyrum estate, a four-bedroomed cottage about a quarter of a mile out of town, which offered them more privacy.

The cottage belonged to Henry Cheape, an old Harrovian, and it offered more privacy for the couple, especially as its two acres were hidden behind a six-foot wall.

OPPOSITE: Kate carries her skis in Klosters in 2005 during her second trip there with Prince William; the possibility of marriage was broached by a media man – William responded by saying "I am only 22 for God's sake! I don't want to get married until I'm at least 28".

LEFT: Prince William skis down the Madrisa slopes, above the Swiss village of Klosters in April 2004. William and Kate's romance became public knowledge during this holiday – and the prince let it be known that he was irritated by the paparrazi shots of him and his new girlfriend.

ABOVE: Flecked with foam, first-year student Kate takes part in the St Andrews Raisin Day, a university tradition to honour the academic family that dates back centuries – originally raisins were used but these days the festivities involve a huge amount of foam instead.

RIGHT: Prince William acknowledges the crowd after graduating at St Andrews in June 2005. As one chapter of his life closed, another was not only gathering pace but getting the thumbs-up, too.

William and Kate's four-year university course ended in June 2005 when the couple graduated at the same ceremony, William with a 2:1 degree in Geography and Kate with a 2:1 in Art History. Charles and Camilla, who had been married at the Guildhall in Windsor just two months earlier, were present along with the Queen and Prince Philip. For the Queen, it was an opportunity to catch her first glimpse of the girl who had captured her grandson's heart.

On the same day, the prince took the opportunity to thank the people of St Andrews, saying he had "thoroughly enjoyed" his four years at the university and was "sad to leave".

"I just want to say a big thank-you to everyone who has made my time here so enjoyable," he said. "I have been able to lead as 'normal' a student life as I could have hoped for and I'm very grateful to everyone, particularly the locals, who have helped make this happen."

He also paid tribute to the Queen, who was recovering from a heavy cold: "Today is a very special day for me and I am delighted that I can share it with my family, and in particular with my grandmother, who has made such an effort to come, having been under the weather."

William and Kate and the royal party also listened to the words of the Vice-Chancellor, Dr Brian Lang, at the end of the ceremony. "You will have made life-long friends," he told the graduates. "You may have met your husband or wife. Our title as the top matchmaking university in Britain signifies so much that is good about St Andrews, so we rely on you to go forth and multiply."

We now know at least one couple took him at his word.

4

A LOW-KEY COURTSHIP

"We moved in together as friends [at St Andrews], we lived with a couple of others as well, and it just sort of blossomed from there, really. We just saw more of each other, hung out a bit more and did stuff."

Prince William

LEFT: William and Kate show a rare display of public affection at an Eton College Old Boys Field Game in 2006.

ABOVE: Kate and her mother Carole show their support for Prince William during a polo game on a windy summer's day in Tetbury, Gloucester, in 2005.

Kate's daring catwalk appearance in March 2002 had made William sit up and take notice of his friend, but it would be a while before romance blossomed.

In the autumn of the same year, Kate was one of a party of 16 friends, including the prince, who stayed at Wood Farm on the Queen's Sandringham estate for a shooting weekend. Long-lens photos of the group taken by local photographers show Kate wreathed in smiles standing next to the prince. They are dressed in jeans, wellington boots and country jackets. Kate has her hands thrust deeply into her pockets, while William holds a shotgun under his arms. The prince's black Labrador completes the picture of a rural idyll. It was the first time that the couple had appeared in the same frame and inevitably fuelled speculation that this young lady was "the one".

In May 2003 the couple were again snapped unawares, this time they were deep in conversation at a rugby sevens match. The same month Kate's father gave a good-natured rebuttal to a journalist's suggestion that his daughter might be dating the future king. "I spoke to Kate just a few days ago," said Michael, "and I can categorically confirm they are no more than good friends. There are two boys and two girls sharing a flat at university. They are together all the time because they are the best of pals and, yes, cameramen are going to get photos of them together. But there is nothing more to it than that."

Michael added, "We're very amused at the thought of being in-laws to Prince William, but I don't think it's going to happen."

A month later, William celebrated his 21st birthday with an "Out of Africa" themed party at Windsor Castle. His uncles, Earl Spencer and the Duke of York, were dressed as big-game hunters and his grandmother was dressed as her African counterpart the Queen of Swaziland, complete with tribal headdress. "I thought it would be fun to see the family out of black ties and get everyone to dress up," he told an interviewer a few days earlier.

His college friends arrived in a white minibus which had a banner draped across it with the words "St Andrews on Safari". There was no mention of Kate in the following day's newspapers as the headlines were dominated by news of the arrest of an intruder, Aaron Barschak, a self-styled "comedy terrorist" who gatecrashed the event and remained undetected until he leaped

ABOVE: Playing to win – and no doubt to impress Kate and her mother, too – William strikes a pose on the field at the Beaufort polo club, Tetbury, Gloucestershire.

on stage in the middle of William's speech and grabbed the microphone before horrified security men realized he wasn't an invited guest and hauled him out of the Great Hall.

The second noteworthy event picked up on was the presence of Jessica Craig, known to her friends as "Jecca", whose family owned a 45,000-acre reserve in Kenya that William has visited on several occasions. It was even suggested that the couple had a "pretend engagement" on a visit he paid to the Craigs during his gap year.

After the Windsor party the prince took the unusual step of denying the romance with Jecca. His spokeswoman announced,

"St James's Palace denies that there is or ever has been any romantic liaison between Prince William and Jessica Craig."

In an interview to mark his milestone birthday, William flatly denied that romance was on the horizon with Kate, Jecca or anybody else. "There's been a lot of speculation about every single girl I'm with, and it actually does quite irritate me after a while, more so because it's a complete pain for the girls.

"These poor girls, whom I've either just met or are friends of mine, suddenly get thrown into the limelight and their parents get rung up and so on.

"If I fancy a girl and she fancies me back, which is rare, I ask her out. But at the same time, I don't want to put them in an awkward situation, because a lot of people don't understand what comes with me, for one – and secondly, if they were my girlfriend, the excitement it would cause."

The exact date when William and Kate's friendship developed into a romance remains uncertain, though it is thought to have been some time towards the end of 2003.

ABOVE: Appearing calm and focused, Kate Middleton takes public transport to a job interview in central London in September 2005 – the publication of this photograph led to her lawyers writing to newspaper and magazine editors asking them to respect her privacy.

It was the following Easter, in April 2004, that it became obvious they were a couple. Paparazzo Jason Fraser, who had broken the news of the Diana and Dodi romance by photographing them kissing on the Al Fayed yacht *Jonikal*, snapped a series of photos of William and Kate in a chairlift at the ski resort of Klosters. The couple are staring fondly at each other and the next morning's *Sun* newspaper carried the photo and the headline: "FINALLY... WILLS GETS A GIRL".

There were few public sightings of the couple during the next year. Kate wasn't invited to the wedding of Prince Charles to Camilla Parker Bowles in April 2005, probably because her presence in front of the world's media would have fuelled expectation that theirs would be the next royal marriage.

Two weeks before the wedding Charles, William and Harry had returned to Klosters for a genteel version of a stag do. On their first night of their Swiss holiday William took the unusual step of having a 30-minute informal chat with journalists during which he spoke about marriage – or the lack of one in his case. "Look, I'm only 22 for God's sake," he told the hacks. "I'm too young to marry at my age. I don't want to get married until I'm at least 28 or maybe 30."

BELOW: It's November 2005 and it's out with public transport and in with a chauffeur-driven car. Kate and William leave her London flat by a means that reflects her soon-to-be-royal status.

The prince will be 28 when he walks down the aisle, so his 2005 casual interview proved to be prescient.

In June 2005 William and Kate attended the wedding of Hugh van Cutsem and Rose Astor at St John's Church in Burford, Oxfordshire. Hugh's parents, Emilie and Hugh senior, are old friends of the Prince of Wales and he and his three brothers, Edward, Nicholas and William, have known William and Harry since the latter were born. As would be their regular practice at the many weddings they have attended over the past five years, William and Kate arrived separately, with a smiling Kate running the gauntlet of photographers as she entered the twelfth-century building. Only later did the couple meet up at Bruern, the Astor home, where they danced intimately together before leaving for a romantic stay at the King's Head in Bledington.

After their graduation there was another romantic break, this time in Kenya. Again there was a separate arrival, with William jetting in from New Zealand following an official tour. It was William's third visit to Lewa Downs, which had been home to Jecca Craig's family since they emigrated there after the First World War. If Kate had had any reservations about William's relationship with their host's daughter they were dispelled during this break during which they were joined by Jecca's new boyfriend, financier Hugh Crossley.

Back in the UK, Kate found herself hounded by the press. In October 2005, following the publication of a photo showing her looking out of the window of a London bus the previous month, her lawyers, the same used by the Prince of Wales, asked newspaper and magazine editors to respect her privacy. Her legal team claimed that photographers had followed her almost every day and night since she left university.

That autumn there were rumours that the relationship had cooled off, but in November William put paid to those when he discussed Kate at a Buckingham Palace reception for the visiting New Zealand All Blacks rugby team. During an exchange of light-hearted banter the lock forward Ali Williams asked the prince how his relationship was doing and was told "going well, going steady".

OPPOSITE: Princes William and Harry take to their skis in Klosters, Switzerland, with Kate in March 2005. The inclusion of William's girlfriend on this break fuelled the rumours of an imminent royal engagement.

RIGHT: *Camilla, Duchess of Cornwall and Prince Charles attend the graduation ceremony of Prince William at Sandhurst. When the couple invited Kate to the Royal box for lunch during the Cheltenham Gold Cup race further rumours of a royal wedding emerged.*

LEFT: *William shares a joke with his grandmother as the Queen inspects his Passing Out parade at the Royal Military Academy, Sandhurst, in December 2006; Kate, her parents and brother Jamie were also guests at the graduation ceremony.*

In January, the couple were once again skiing in Klosters. Despite knowing there must have been cameras spying on their every move in the popular resort, William planted a kiss on Kate's cheek and, sure enough, the photo was splashed across the front pages.

Days later William began his army training at the Royal Military Academy, Sandhurst, and the romance was virtually on hold yet again. This earned his girlfriend the title "Waity Katie" for her seemingly endless ability to stand by her man, and put her own future on hold while his progressed steadily.

The pair met up the weekend before Valentine's Day, but the break ended up as something of a disaster after they joined William's cousins Peter and Zara Phillips and William's old friend Guy Pelly for a night out. The group met at the Tunnel House

Inn, in the village of Coates, near Cirencester, a 15-minute drive from Highgrove. Pelly was secretly filmed smoking cannabis, which he denied possessing, saying that he had been offered it by a girl in the pub and had thought it was a cigarette. William and Kate weren't involved but there were questions raised about the company they were keeping.

In March, Kate arrived on her own to watch National Hunt's most prestigious race, the Cheltenham Gold Cup. In a telling gesture, she was invited to the Royal Box for lunch with Prince Charles and the Duchess of Cornwall and was later photographed with the royal party on the balcony overlooking the racecourse. It was the first time she had been seen in public with her future in-laws and, given that Prince William wasn't even present, it was a sign that she was definitely part of the family. Later in the day she watched the races with Camilla's children Tom and Laura and their partners.

There was another sign the romance was blossoming when Kate turned up at Eton College to watch William play in the

LEFT: Kate stands out from the crowd at William's Passing Out parade at Sandhurst in December 2006. Now that he had graduated from Sandhurst, the question on everyone's minds was, would she still be "Waity Katie"?

old boys' Eton Field Game match. She embraced him in front of guests and playfully ruffled his thinning locks.

A month later, the couple flew to Mustique which had been a favourite holiday destination of the prince's great aunt Princess Margaret. She'd had a villa, Les Jolies Eaux, built for her on land given to her as a wedding present from her life-long friend Lord Glenconner.

William and Kate plus a group of friends stayed in a five-bedroomed villa belonging to Belle and John Robinson the owners of the Jigsaw fashion chain. Set in the hillside 250 ft above sea level, the Villa Hibiscus overlooks Macaroni Beach and offers unparalled views of the sea and other Caribbean islands.

While they were there they met up with Richard Branson and played several games of tennis with the Virgin Group boss, whose daughter Holly is a friend of the royal couple. They also went to Firefly, a fashionable guesthouse, where Zara Phillips has stayed, and ordered cocktails. Another holidaymaker said, "They were very nice and ordinary. They watched the sunset and had

ABOVE: The beginning of an intense media fury with rumours of an imminent engagement to Prince William reaching fever pitch, Kate is pictured here on her 25th birthday, leaving her Chelsea home besieged by photographers.

ABOVE: William's girlfriend was continually pursued by paparazzi, something the prince was acutely aware of – and was a possible factor in their break-up in 2007.

LEFT: Kate only had to step out of her door to be followed by the paparazzi and the signs of stress were beginning to show.

two drinks each, signing them to the Villa Hibiscus account."

The couple also visited Basil's Bar, a local bistro that was a great favourite of Margaret's. "On karaoke night the prince and two of his friends sang Elvis Presley's 'Suspicious Minds'," a staff member later recalled. "The prince drank his favourite vodka and cranberry juice while Kate enjoyed a piña colada flavoured with St Vincent's own blend of rum, Sunset Premium."

On their return, they attended the Wiltshire wedding of Camilla's daughter Laura to Harry Lopes, grandson of the late Lord Astor of Hever. As usual, Kate arrived after William, but her presence at a family wedding once again fuelled speculation that a more royal one was imminent.

During the second half of the year, Kate was devastated by the loss of her two grandmothers, Carole's mother Dorothy Goldsmith succumbed to cancer in July at the age of 71 and Kate read a poem at her funeral. Then Michael's mother Valerie died from lymphoma in September at the age of 82. Her widower Peter died just a week before William and Kate announced their engagement in November 2010.

ABOVE: Looking close, Prince William and Kate watch the RBS Six Nations Championship rugby match between England and Italy at Twickenham a couple of months before their split; Prince Harry, meantime, appears somewhat non-plussed.

LEFT: Kate lets her hair down, but keeps up appearances leaving the high-end Mahiki nightclub, London in February of 2007 wearing a knee-length printed silk dress by New York designer BCBG Max Azria.

To cheer Kate up, William arranged for them to charter a yacht with some friends off the holiday island of Ibiza. Photos show them happy and relaxed as they dived into the sea, and at one point they all appear to be enjoying a mud bath.

In December 2006, Kate and her parents and brother James were William's guests at his graduation ceremony at Sandhurst that was also attended by Charles, Camilla, Prince Philip and the Queen. Instead of walking from the car park with other families, Kate's party walked down the ceremonial routeway that was lined with troops for Her Majesty's arrival. It was the highest profile event that Kate had attended so far and was seen as proof that the royal romance was rock solid.

No one watching that day could have realized that behind the public smiles their love affair was in fact starting to flounder and that four months later the couple would separate.

5
BREAK-UP

❧

> "They've been scrutinised constantly, comments made, editorials written about a relationship they themselves are probably trying to figure out. We talk about how difficult it is for people who become a celebrity overnight, but for her, it was worse. It wasn't what she was looking for, she just fell in love with a boy she met at college."

Psychologist Dr Linda Papadopoulos

LEFT: Kate and Prince William strike an awkward pose at the Cheltenham horse-racing festival in March 2007, and with good reason – within weeks the couple went their separate ways.

S peculation of an imminent engagement had been rife since November 2006 when the now defunct High Street chain Woolworths produced a range of memorabilia, including souvenir plates, mugs, thimbles and mouse mats, to mark the event.

Beneath portraits of the couple on the designs was the message "Celebrating the Royal Marriage of William and Kate" with a space left underneath for the date – across the top of the design was emblazoned the year, which simply said "2007", implying the wedding would be the following year. Prince William was said to be "horrified" by the media hype the story created.

In the New Year, the rumours gathered momentum as Kate's

ABOVE: Demure rather than dashing, Kate and Prince William go through the motions at the Cheltenham Festival of March 2007; this was the last time the couple were pictured together before it emerged that they had separated in mid-April.

RIGHT: *Looking crestfallen, Kate walks back into her parents' home in Bucklebury, Berkshire, the day after her split with Prince William was announced on 14 April 2007.*

25th birthday approached on January 9. Patrick Jephson, Diana's former Private Secretary, wrote a feature for *The Spectator* entitled "The Next People's Princess" in which he suggested that the royal family was about to get "a much-needed injection of fresh young glamour".

Kate was used to one or two photographers waiting to snap her as she left her Chelsea flat, but on the morning of her birthday a few days later there were dozens outside, eagerly

awaiting a timely announcement. For William it was all too reminiscent of the hounding his mother had received in the run-up to her marriage, and his office issued a statement condemning the harassment Kate was receiving. "He wants more than anything for it to stop," said his Press Officer. "Miss Middleton should, like any other private individual, be able to go about her everyday business without this kind of intrusion. The situation is proving unbearable for all those concerned."

William was now based with the Household Cavalry at

LEFT: Life goes on – Prince WIlliam heads away from his brother's leaving for Iraq party at the end of April. Prince Harry had been scheduled for deployment to the front line within weeks, a decision that was subsequently reversed for safety reasons.

Combermere Barracks in Windsor. There were the occasional meetings with Kate in London, including a visit to Twickenham to watch England beat Italy in the Six Nations Cup. However, by now much of the spark had gone out of the relationship. Kate was upset that William had pulled out of holidaying with the Middletons in Scotland to mark the New Year, and William was finding himself pulled in two different directions with the need to make a good impact in his new role in the army and his need to keep his relationship with Kate on course.

The couple booked a holiday in the exclusive Swiss resort of Zermatt, but William invited along some of his friends, including Guy Pelly and Thomas Van Straubenzee. Having hardly seen William since Christmas, Kate found it frustrating that they now had no opportunity to be alone to talk things through. Paparazzi

ABOVE: Pale and drawn, yet still under the full glare of the media, Kate is driven away from her parents' home a few days after the break-up of the royal romance.

photos of the group at an open-air lunch show them at opposite ends of the table with both of them looking dejected.

Things got worse on their return when they attended the first day of the Cheltenham Festival on 13 March 2007 which would prove to be the last time they were photographed together in public until later in the summer. While Kate managed a forced smile, William looked distinctly out of sorts.

The following day's headlines included "Fred and Gladys Mark II" – a reference to the jokey nicknames Charles and Camilla once gave each other. Much was made out of the fact that the young couple's wardrobes made them look jaded and older than their years. "Miss Middleton's snug jacket and long skirt could have come straight from Camilla's wardrobe," said one report, adding, "and that demure clasping of hands is certainly a favourite Camilla pose." William fared no better: "At 24 he looked like a younger version of his 58-year-old father."

Three days later, William moved to Dorset to begin a ten-week tank-commander course at Bovington army training camp. It was too far for him to visit the capital regularly at weekends, but it didn't stop him letting his hair down with his new army buddies.

The group visited Elements nightclub in Bournemouth at the end of the month. The normally cautious William was happy to pose for snaps taken on mobile phones. Some of these were later splashed across the tabloids, much to Kate's anger and his embarrassment. In one, he appears to be holding the breast of Brazilian Ana Ferreira who later told *The Sun*, "There were a lot of girls hanging around him and he was posing for pictures. He had me on one arm and my friend Cecilia on the other. I was a little bit drunk myself, but I felt something brush my breast. I thought it couldn't be the future king but now I've seen the picture, it's no wonder he's got a smile on his face."

The *Sunday Mirror* carried a similar story a few days later in which 19-year-old Lisa Agar, who had been at the same club, recalled William "being very flirty. I was quite taken aback but just went for it. He was laughing his head off and waving his hands in the air".

Later a friend of the prince invited the girls back to the barracks. They sat for 20 minutes or so in the lounge area of the

ABOVE: *Kate is joined by her sister Pippa at a London book launch a month after splitting up with Prince William.*

OPPOSITE: *Sporting sunglasses, a dark blue jumper, white skirt and boots, Kate remains in the public spotlight at the Badminton Horse Trials in May 2007.*

RIGHT: There's definitely more than a hint of "look what you're missing, William" as Kate hits the town during May; here she is seen leaving the exclusive Boujis nightclub in Kensington.

LEFT: Wearing a regimental tie and traditional bowler hat, Prince William attends the Cavalry Old Comrades Association Annual Parade in London's Hyde Park in May 2007.

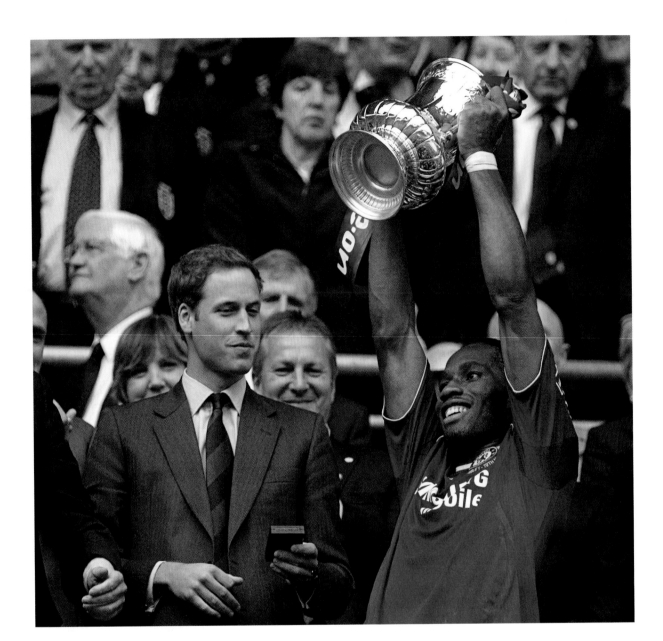

camp before the girls left. Ms Agar ends her account by saying "Strangely I felt a bit sorry for William and I thought maybe he was cheering himself up".

William and Kate's final night out together was a quiet one with friends Hugh and Rose van Cutsem, whose wedding in Burford they had attended in 2005. The four enjoyed a drink in the King's Head pub in Bledington. The couple's last meeting together after this was during the Easter weekend when they finally decided to call it a day.

News of the break-up appeared in the tabloids on Saturday 14 April and the same day Kate was photographed looking tense

ABOVE: Prince William, in his role as president of the English Football Association, looks on as Chelsea's Didier Drogba hoists the FA Cup at Wembley; Drogba's strike settled the 2007 Final as Chelsea beat Portsmouth 1–0.

RIGHT: In the weeks after the split with William, Kate hit the nightclub scene; here she is pictured returning home after a night out in London.

and drawn as she walked from the car into her parents' house.

The Sunday newspapers analysed what could have gone wrong, with many of them unfairly highlighting the Middleton family's middle-class background as a possible reason. William's friends had apparently quipped "doors to manual" at the mention of Carole, a reference to her air stewardess days. It was suggested that the royals took a dim view of her chewing gum at William's passing out parade at Sandhurst, although it was later pointed out that she was in fact chewing the nicotine

LEFT: William plays polo for Team Umbogo in the Chakravarty Cup at Ham Polo Club, Richmond, in mid-June 2007; the event helped to raise funds for the Centrepoint charity

variety to wean herself off cigarettes. Comments that Carole had said, "Pleased to meet you" on meeting the Queen and had referred to the lavatory as "the toilet" were petty; what's more, her supposed remarks seem unlikely since it is not even confirmed that the Middletons had met the monarch at that stage.

William, who had great respect for the Middleton family and had always enjoyed his visits to Bucklebury, rang Kate to tell her that neither he nor his "friends" referred to in the accounts, had ever said anything as vitriolic.

In previous generations when the royals split from a partner, there would be no contact afterwards. After a 16-year

OPPOSITE: Wearing a black top and a long floral skirt, Kate arrives home after a racy night out at the Kitts Club in London's Sloane Square in early June 2007

relationship socialite Freda Dudley Ward only found out that she been dumped by the future King Edward VIII when he instructed his switchboard not to put her calls through. "I'm most dreadfully sorry," the telephonist told her, "but I have orders never to put you through again."

With mutual friends plus a shared past that included their time at university, it would have been against the grain for William to emulate his great-great-uncle, and he seems to have kept in touch with Kate throughout their split.

This period in their relationship, unsurprisingly, seems to have had a profound effect on them, and they spoke about it

ABOVE: Duty calls, even after a break-up – Prince William (centre) watches the 2007 Trooping the Colour parade from the Buckingham Palace balcony with (from left) Prince Andrew, Princess Beatrice, The Queen and Prince Philip.

openly and at length during their interview with Tom Bradby on the day of their engagement. Kate admitted that she had been angry about it at the time but she said that she now looked back on it as a positive experience and admitted she had been "consumed" with the relationship.

The Prince said they had needed "space" at the time but he had always known Kate was "very special".

"I wouldn't believe everything you read in the paper but in that particular instance we did split up for a bit," he said. "We were both very young… and we were both defining ourselves as such and being different characters. It was very much trying to find our way and we were growing up. It was just a bit of space, things like that, and things worked out for the better."

Kate added: "I, at the time, wasn't very happy about it but actually it made me a stronger person. You find out things about yourself that maybe you hadn't realized. You can get quite consumed by a relationship when you are younger. I really valued that time, for me as well… looking back on it."

At the time, however, the newly single William wasted no time in hitting the nightclubs again, enjoying a late night drink at Bliss wine bar in Bournemouth and, on the eve of the story breaking in the newspapers, he was at Mahiki, in London's Mayfair, one of his favourite haunts. At the latter, the royal party quaffed £450 bottles of vintage Dom Pérignon champagne and William is supposed to have yelled "I'm free" as he took to the dance floor. His bill for his first night of "freedom" in the capital was a princely £4,700.

Meanwhile Kate may have been angry, but she wasn't about to mope. The week after the split, she and her mother Carole went to Dublin to attend a private exhibition of paintings by Gemma Billington, in the Hanover Quay area of the city. They also toured the National Gallery of Ireland.

Back in England, she herself took onto the London nightclub scene. Always friendly and polite to the press, she seemed to be making more of an effort than ever to co-operate, with the result that the photos of her splashed across the papers were of a carefree, happy and undoubtedly sexy girl about town, rather than a pining Miss Havisham figure. Her dresses were shorter and slinkier than before, and for once she

ABOVE: During June 2007 William – pictured here at the Beaufort Polo Club, Gloucestershire – and his brother Harry were heavily involved in the planning of the Concert for Diana, a charity event at Wembley that involved a host of the world's leading entertainers and musicians.

was using more than her share of fake tan. The new Kate's behaviour was reminiscent of Diana's, who memorably turned up at the Serpentine Gallery wearing a short and sassy black cocktail dress the night Charles was set to admit his adultery in an interview by Jonathan Dimbleby for an ITV documentary. Diana's Christina Stambolian outfit was called "Di's Revenge Dress" or, more crudely, her "Up Yours Frock". Either way, it knocked Charles's admission of adultery off the next morning's front pages. The Kate couture of April and May 2007 had a similar "see what you're missing" message for William.

Kate also made headlines when she took part in a new charity venture. Alice Fox Pitt, a friend from Kate's Marlborough days, had organized the Sisterhood, a group of 21 girls who aimed to row a Dragon boat from Dover to the French coast to raise money for charity. Emma Sayle, who was in charge of the project, recounted her memories of the event to royal biographer

ABOVE: Prince William, sitting in the front row alongside his brother, is two rows away from Kate (far right, in conversation with her brother James). William and Kate barely exchanged glances during the six-hour music extravaganza, but were inseparable at the after-show party.

OPPOSITE: Kate and her brother James arrive for the Concert for Diana at Wembley on 1 July 2007. The event, staged on what would have been Diana's 46th birthday, raised funds for charities such as the Diana Princess of Wales Memorial Fund, Centrepoint and Sentebale.

Katie Nicholl: "Kate was very down and I think the training became her therapy. Kate had always put William first and she said this was a chance to do something for herself." The training sessions took place on the Thames at Chiswick and gradually they became a magnet for photographers who eagerly joined the crew for the 6.30 am starts.

By now, she had resumed her affair with William, although it wasn't common knowledge. The clue came later when Kate pulled out of training. Newspaper accounts at the time suggested she was under pressure from Clarence House to withdraw, as the media interest was growing daily. The couple had got back together after William had invited her to an end-of-training party in his barracks on 9 June. It ended with them kissing on the dance floor and it was reported she stayed overnight in his quarters.

ABOVE: All smiles at Wembley stadium! Although Kate and William kept their distance, publicly at least, during the Concert for Diana, the couple had in fact already got back together.

*ABOVE: Prince William talks to
members of Take That backstage
after they had performed three songs
at the Concert for Diana in July
2007.*

The first the world at large knew of the rekindled romance was at the Concert for Diana, held at Wembley Stadium on 1 July 2007 on what would have been William's mother's 46th birthday. It was one of the events that Princes William and Harry had planned to mark the tenth anniversary of her death. The concert featured 23 acts and raised £1.6 million for charity.

Kate and William sat two rows apart and never exchanged a glance during the evening – but at the after-show party they were inseparable. A snatched photo of them taken with a mobile phone shows them deep in conversation, over a candle-lit supper. The message was clear: the romance was back on.

ABOVE: Performers Natasha Bedingfield, Sir Tom Jones and Joss Stone are flanked by Princes William and Harry during the post-concert celebrations.

RIGHT: Training with the Sisterhood gave Kate a new focus, and by the time she ultimately pulled out of the charity project – rowing from Dover to the French coast in August – she and William had been secretly dating again for several weeks.

6

A FIRMER
FOOTING

✦

"They're very much in love. They're very tactile, they're very good together, he makes her laugh, she makes him laugh, and I think also, dare I say, that she kind of slightly rules the roost!"

Fox News royal correspondent Neil Sean in January 2009

LEFT: Kate and William attend the wedding of friends Harry Meade and Rosemarie Bradford in October 2010; Kate's stunning blue dress by London design house Issa, chic black jacket and wide-brimmed hat drew admiring glances, but the couple, fresh from a safari in Kenya, were hiding a big secret – the prince had proposed marriage while they were away, and Kate had accepted.

ABOVE: Kate and her sister Pippa leave Windsor after watching Prince William play rugby.

Any doubts that the royal romance was back on were dispelled later in the month when Kate was invited to Camilla's 60th birthday party at Highgrove.

An invitation to the black- tie event, held on Saturday 21 July 2007, four days after the actual anniversary, was hastily despatched to Kate and although she was holidaying with friends in the Caribbean she said she was "hopeful" of being there.

Camilla had been keen to invite her all along as she had always got on well with Kate, but it had to be William's decision in the end. The prince was adamant that she should be there but he was equally determined not to upstage his step-mother's big day, so Kate was smuggled in through a private driveway to the estate. The photographers at the main entrance, all hoping to catch a glimpse of Kate, had to make do with other VIP arrivals. The Princess Royal drove from her nearby Gatcombe estate with husband Tim Laurence and ex-King Constantine of Greece. Her daughter Zara followed with boyfriend Mike Tindall, and a host of celebrity friends of Charles and Camilla's attended the event including Sir David Frost, Joan Rivers, Joanna Lumley, Stephen Fry, Prunella Scales and her husband Timothy West.

Kate wore a stunning full-length cream dress and appeared happy and relaxed as she sipped champagne in the beautiful gardens. The 200 guests enjoyed a three-course organic dinner, and after speeches they took to the dance floor. Kate was said to be "draped" over her boyfriend of four years, and William mouthed the words of the Frank Sinatra classic "It Had to Be You" to his girlfriend.

Ironically, the same month that she was the belle of Camilla's ball, Kate was named the most sought-after party guest in town by *Tatler*. "Suddenly single, this sexy siren is super in-demand. Life after Wills is rather better than you'd imagine," trumpeted the magazine, little realizing that a) the couple were again an item; and b) her London partying days were now self-rationed and from hence forward the couple would go to great lengths to avoid being seen in public.

It was also during this year that Kate began to receive plaudits for her fashion sense, and there were, and continue to be, obvious parallels drawn with the woman who would have been Kate's mother-in-law. In July 2006, UK *Vogue* editor

RIGHT: The photo that proved that
William and Kate were back together.
Pictured here in Windsor Great Park
on a pheasant shoot – a Christmas gift
from the Queen – the couple were
later seen hugging and kissing.

Alexandra Shulman wrote, "Kate is a contemporary version of
Princess Diana. She has the same mainstream style and will go on
like Diana to get more glamorous."

As Britain marked the tenth anniversary of Diana's death in
the summer of 2007, David Emanuel, the man who designed
Diana's wedding dress with his then wife Elizabeth, also noted
similarities between the two women. "Kate seems to be a very
cool girl. She has a very polished look, without too much
make-up, and her hair is always very glossy and shiny. She
always shows a lot of leg, which is fine because her legs are a
good feature. She is tall, which is helpful to carry off the clothes
she wears. She is always picture perfect and royal almost to the
manner born."

Fellow designer Bruce Oldfield first met the shy 19-year-old
Diana Spencer on the eve of her marriage to the Prince of Wales.
"When she started she didn't have a clue," he later recalled.
"She was a little country bumpkin, a typical Sloane, with
cardigans and Laura Ashley see-through skirts. She wasn't at all
sophisticated like Kate is now."

LEFT: William becomes the latest member of the royal family to earn his Royal Air Force "wings". Kate joins him at the graduation ceremony in Lincolnshire in April 2008. The previous day William attended the 90th anniversary dinner of the RAF.

For the House of Windsor, it is a plus that Kate also plays it safe in the sartorial stakes. Her style is as discreet as her personality: attractive, classy, always appropriate for the occasion and with just the hint of quirkiness.

Both women took fashion advice to improve their look: Diana from *Vogue's* Anna Harvey and Kate from stylist Leesa Whisker, who reportedly became her personal shopper and was responsible for helping choose the turquoise BCBG gown that Kate wore to the Boodles Boxing Ball, a charity fundraiser, in June 2006.

By 2007 it was clear that Kate could be a leader of fashion as long as she remained in the limelight. When she wore a £40 Topshop black-and-white tunic dress on her 25th birthday, it sold out the next morning.

As future Queen, Kate would be a terrific asset to the fashion industry if she followed the traditional Buy British route that royal ladies have favoured. Esteemed fashion director of the *Daily Telegraph* Hilary Alexander says, "Hopefully she will come out of the closet and be an ambassador for fashion. It would be great if she adopted young designers such as Richard

LEFT: Enjoying a joke together with friends, Kate and William enjoy the polo on his 26th birthday.

Nicoll, Jonathan Saunders or Christopher Kane. Someone with her profile could give British fashion a boost across the world."

In August, the couple holidayed on Desroches Island, in the Seychelles. It was an opportunity for the two to be alone – apart from the inevitable personal detectives – in what would be their first overseas holiday since January 2006. Here it is reckoned that the couple made a pact. Kate needed reassurance that the romance was going places, and William needed to know that he could concentrate on his career – he still had to spend another six months' deployment with the RAF and the Royal Navy. Marriage would be on the cards, but it would be a way off yet.

Such arrangements are not unusual in royal circles. The Queen, as Princess Elizabeth, was besotted by Lieutenant Philip Mountbatten, another serviceman, and at the same time faced tremendous pressure from her parents not to put all her eggs in one basket and to consider other suitors as well. According to Philip, in conversation with an authorized biographer, the couple came to "an understanding" in the autumn of 1946, although they only became officially engaged the following July. William and Kate reached a similar "understanding" on the holiday

LEFT: Sheltering from the inclement weather and the media, William, Kate and Harry tuck in to William's birthday picnic while watching the Williams De Brou Test Match at Beaufort Polo Club.

island of Desroches, that marriage would definitely take place, though as we now know, the actual date would be a fair way down the line.

Back in the UK, William had to put the finishing touches to the memorial service held at Wellington Barracks on 31 August 2007, to mark the tenth anniversary of his mother's death. Kate didn't attend and, after a vitriolic war of words in the media, Camilla was also absent on the day. It was an intense occasion for Diana's sons. Prince Harry gave a moving address, telling the packed congregation, "When she was alive we completely took for granted her unrivalled love of life, laughter, fun and folly." In a voice breaking with emotion, he added, "She will always be

ABOVE: Proud parents, Carole and Michael, pose with Kate's sister, Pippa Middleton, on her graduation day at Edinburgh University; Kate did not attend.

remembered for her amazing public work. But behind the media glare, to us, she was quite simply the best mother in the world."

In a gesture that would have delighted Diana, William sat with the royal family, while Harry sat on the right side of the church with the Spencers, a healing gesture after a decade of division that began with Earl Spencer's funeral eulogy which captured the public mood at the time, but which went against the royal grain of keeping feelings buttoned up and private.

The long-awaited inquest into the deaths of Diana, Princess of Wales and Dodi Al Fayed opened on 2 October 2007. For William and Harry it must have been traumatic to say the least since it dealt with questions such as "Was Diana pregnant at the time of her death?" and "Were the British security services involved in her death?"

Dodi's father Mohamed Al Fayed, convinced that his son was deliberately killed, set the dramatic tone of the inquest on his way into court, telling reporters, "At last we're going to have a jury from ordinary people and I hope to reach the decision which I believe, that my son and Princess Diana have been murdered by the Royal Family."

The day after, William and Kate were spotted enjoying a dinner date in Locanda Ottoemezzo, a popular Italian eaterie in Thackeray Street, a few hundred yards from his childhood home at Kensington Palace. For once there were no friends there, the ever-present paparazzi hadn't been tipped off about it, and the prince's detectives sat outside in a car to give the couple more privacy.

They sat side by side at a small table, their faces close together in the candlelight, and at one point William cradled Kate's face in his hands as they chatted in low voices.

A couple of days later the two were photographed together leaving Boujis nightclub at 2.00 am. For the photographers waiting outside it was a golden opportunity to snap the media-avoiding pair together and they chased William's Range Rover as it set off from Thurloe Street in South Kensington back to Clarence House. Given that it was the week in which the Diana inquest was examining the car chase that lead to her death, this episode was all the more upsetting for the prince. The following day Clarence House complained about the antics of the press

ABOVE: A favourite past-time and a much-loved destination for the royals: Kate and William ski side-by-side in Klosters in March 2008; they were later joined by Prince Charles at the Swiss resort.

RIGHT: Happy and relaxed: William and Kate take a stroll at Coworth Park, Ascot in May 2009; the couple enjoyed a post-match drink after William and his brother Harry had played polo.

and William was said to find the photographers' behaviour "incomprehensible".

Others begged to differ, and some commentators pointed out that a newsworthy tale such as the second in line to the throne publicly out on the town with his girlfriend after a split was a legitimate story. The Queen herself was apparently unimpressed that her grandson should go to a high-profile venue when he knew it was almost certain he would be photographed. The Duke of Edinburgh suggested that his grandson should avoid Boujis in future.

Less than a week after the Press contretemps outside Boujis, Kate was again snapped by the paparazzi, this time in Scotland, when she and the prince stayed with Prince Charles at Birkhall. Kate proved that, unlike Diana who hated being "dragged" to the Deeside estate, she was really at home with the royal family's shooting, hunting and fishing lifestyle. Wearing a camouflage jacket, dark jeans, leg warmers and gaiters over her boots, she could be seen at one point lying on the ground preparing the sights of her gun before firing. The Prince of Wales, dressed in a waterproof jacket, stood nearby supervising proceedings.

The intimate family scene once again fuelled talk of an engagement. Bookmakers were, by this time, so sure of an announcement that they stopped taking bets on whether it would happen.

ABOVE: A rare photo of Kate kissing and cuddling her prince after a romantic meal at the Potting Shed Pub in Wiltshire in July 2009 – not surprisingly such intimacy led to further speculation about the pair's future plans.

OPPOSITE: On the final day of his unofficial visit to Australia in January 2010, Prince William arrives at Government House to a mass of adoring fans and wannabe princesses – it was the first time William had returned to Australia since going there with his parents when he was just nine months old.

7
CAREERS

"The time I spent with the RAF earlier this year made me realize how much I love flying. Joining Search and Rescue is a perfect opportunity for me to serve in the Forces operationally, while contributing to a vital part of the country's Emergency Services."

Prince William, September 2008

LEFT: Undergoing military helicopter training at RAF Shawbury in June 2009, William is all set to be a fully operational Search and Rescue pilot for the RAF.

Kate celebrated her 26th birthday, as she had the previous one, without her boyfriend. In 2007 William had been on duty with the Household Cavalry. A year later, he was serving with the RAF at Cranwell.

As King William V, he will one day be Head of the Armed Services and during his apprenticeship years he was determined to serve in all three branches. On 7 January 2008, after seeing in the New Year with Kate on the Balmoral estate, the prince arrived at the base to begin his four-month attachment to Cranwell's Central Flying School. Two days later, Kate marked her princeless birthday by visiting Tom Aikens' restaurant in Elystan Street, Chelsea with her parents and sister Pippa.

In March, Kate made her third appearance at the Cheltenham Festival in as many years. It was exactly 12 months since her

RIGHT: A solemn-looking Kate leaves her London flat in July 2007 on her way to work at Jigsaw; at the time she and William were not together.

BELOW: Fashion brand Jigsaw's headquarters in Kew, west London. After less than a year Kate quit her job as an accessories buyer – a role that had been specially created for her.

ABOVE: A cheerful Prince William greets Naval families in Churchill Square, Helensbrough, Scotland.

tweedy appearance with William had heralded the temporary end of their relationship. Now she was back to more jaunty chic with a navy blue raincoat and matching trilby as she arrived with Thomas van Straubenzee as an escort.

Two days later, she and William flew to Klosters for a skiing trip. This time they ignored the five-star Hotel Walserhof and rented an isolated apartment, where Prince Charles joined them later in the week.

April was a month of contrasting emotions for William. The Diana inquest finally came to an end on the seventh, ten-and-a-half years after his mother's death. A jury decided that Diana was unlawfully killed by the "gross negligence" of the paparazzi who had chased the car carrying the princess and Dodi Al Fayed, and by the driver Henri Paul who had been drinking. In a statement issued on the same day as the verdict was announced, William and Harry thanked the jury for the "thorough way in which they have considered the evidence." They added: "We agree with their verdicts."

At times the princes were appalled at details of the role played by the photographers on the night in question. Undoubtedly it has coloured their attitude to the press. When Harry was forced to return from Afghanistan after details of his deployment had been leaked in the press, he arrived back at RAF Brize Norton barely able to conceal his anger from the waiting media. Similarly, William has tried his best over the years to ensure that Kate never has to go through the same sort of pressure from photographers with which his mother had to cope.

During the spring and summer of 2008, Kate attended four high-profile events in relatively quick succession that left no one in doubt that her position as royal girlfriend was definitely that of a princess-in-waiting, a phrase that began to be used time and again.

On 11 April she made her first appearance at a royal engagement since William's Sandhurst graduation 16 months earlier. On that occasion she hadn't been photographed together with the prince. Now she was filmed walking through RAF Cranwell side by side with him. It was presumed that she would attend the event, although her name was not on any official operations notes beforehand, and she slipped in through a private entrance with William's aunt, Lady Sarah McCorquodale.

She watched William and 25 other newly qualified pilots receive their "wings" from the Prince of Wales before she joined the two princes and the Duchess of Cornwall for a private reception and lunch with the other graduates and senior staff.

Kate was dressed in one of her favourite colour combinations, an ivory-coloured double-breasted coat and black suede calf-length boots. One journalist noted, "She looked slightly apprehensive when she saw the cameras, staring straight ahead and not posing; she swept her hair back from her face which is something she always does when she is nervous."

After William successfully completed his intensive flying course, his instructor, Wing Commander Andy Lowell said, "William was very good. I was very impressed by his flying skills. He had a natural ability and was quick to learn." Flight

Lieutenant Simon Berry who was on the same course added, "William was socializing with everyone. He was just a normal bloke, a normal guy and very sociable."

Unfortunately the kudos earned by the prince for his enthusiasm and commitment was offset when it was leaked that his flight training exercises in a Chinook helicopter involved flights to the family home, Highgrove, and to Sandringham, the Queen's Norfolk estate, as well as landing in the grounds of the Middletons' family home in Berkshire. Although these were justified by the MoD in turn as "a general handling exercise", "low-level flying training" and "practising take-off and landing skills", it was hard not to see them as mere jollies. Worse was to come when it was revealed that the prince had used the Chinook to attend a wedding in Northumberland and, after picking up Harry on the way, also took the chopper to the Isle of Wight for their cousin Peter Phillips' stag party.

Peter's wedding a month later, on 17 May, was Kate's second high-profile event. Nearly all the royal family were present at St George's Chapel, Windsor, although one significant absentee was William who honoured a long-standing commitment to attend the wedding in Kenya of Batian Craig, Jecca's brother, to Melissa Duveen. The prince's gesture proved how very close he had remained to the Craigs and was in part to thank them for the many holidays he had enjoyed with them, enabling him to escape from the press and public scrutiny in the family's wildlife reserve in the foothills of Mount Kenya.

Another month on, and Kate was present, again at St George's Chapel, to watch the procession of garter knights walk from the state apartments of Windsor Castle and through the Lower Ward to the chapel. The Order of the Garter is Britain's oldest order of chivalry and William was greatly touched that his grandmother had made him the 1,000th knight.

His grandfather once said of this event, "It's a nice piece of pageantry which I think a lot of people enjoy. Rationally it's lunatic but, in practice, everyone enjoys it, I think." William looked self-conscious in his velvet robes and ostrich-plumed hat as he processed past his girlfriend who was watching from the Galilee Porch. Prince Harry, roaring with laughter, stood next to her, clearly relishing his brother's acute embarrassment.

ABOVE: Remembrance Sunday 2007 sees Prince William placing a wreath at the Cenotaph in Whitehall for the first time, a sign of his deep respect for the military.

OPPOSITE: William gives a reading at a service celebrating his grandparents' diamond wedding anniversary at Westminster Abbey. Other members of the royal family also attended the November 2007 service.

ABOVE: In a stunning floor-length dress by London design house, Issa, Kate attends the Boodles Boxing Ball in London, in support of Starlight Children's Foundation.

OPPOSITE: William towers over his father at an RAF wings Graduation Ceremony in April 2008 – at 6 ft 3 in William would be the tallest-ever British monarch.

Kate's fourth royal event was another wedding. Lady Rose Windsor, the 28-year-old daughter of the Queen's cousin, the Duke of Gloucester, married George Gilman at the Queen's Chapel, next to St James's Palace on 19 July. Kate looked cool and elegant in a light-blue jacket complementing her multi-coloured silk skirt. In her long flowing hair she wore a black fascinator, that mainstay of modern royal headgear. For once the fashion editors were not concentrating on Miss Middleton but on William's aunt, the Princess Royal, who at 57 arrived wearing the same outfit she wore at Charles and Diana's wedding when she was 31, an abject lesson in royal frugality.

Once again William was absent, this time on board HMS *Iron Duke* on patrol in the Caribbean, as a part of his five-week placement with the Royal Navy. His short stint turned into a bit of a *Boy's Own* adventure. He helped plan exercises to assess the Navy's preparedness should a category five storm hit the volcanic island of Montserrat. Even more exciting was Sub Lt Wales's involvement in a drugs bust when *Iron Duke*, working with the US Coast Guard, seized 45 bales of cocaine valued at £40 million from a speedboat, north-east of Barbados.

Afterwards the ship's captain, Cdr Mark Newland, praised William's maturity and contribution during the seizure, saying "He is a very professional military officer, and very astute".

It had been speculated that William would leave the armed forces in 2009 to become a full-time working royal. In September 2008, Clarence House issued a surprise announcement that the prince intended to train with the RAF Search and Rescue. The course would last 18 months and, if he successfully qualified, he would be committed to serve a unit for three years. The prince's office was keen to point out that he would also still work for the charities and organizations with which he was involved and that he would also undertake some royal duties.

The prince himself said that part of the reason for this change of direction was the fact that, unlike his brother, he was not allowed to serve on the front line: "I now want to build on the experience and training I have received to serve operationally – especially because, for good reasons, I was not able to deploy to Afghanistan this year with D Squadron of the Household Cavalry Regiment."

William was committing himself to the RAF until 2013 and what, queried royal commentators, would that mean about that other pressing commitment – his wedding to Kate?

While the prince's future was being mapped out, there was still no sign of his girlfriend pursuing a long-term, challenging career. She had quit her job as an accessories buyer for fashion chain Jigsaw in November 2007 after working there for less than a year. The job had been created especially for her by owners John and Belle Robinson and it allowed her the flexibility to maintain her relationship with William.

Belle Robinson found her very unassuming and admired her attitude to the other staff and commented about her attitude, which she found quite relaxed: "She sat in the kitchen at lunchtime and chatted with everyone from the van drivers to the accounts girls. She wasn't precious."

The Queen, 85 in April 2011, still undertakes almost 400 engagements a year and was reportedly concerned that Kate was giving herself a work-shy image.

Kate has been involved with one or two charity ventures. In September 2008, she helped to organize a charity roller disco at the Renaissance Rooms in Vauxhall, in aid of Tom's Ward at Oxford's Children's Hospital. The Middleton sisters were happy to join in the fun. Kate wore yellow hot pants and a green sparkly top, and at one point was photographed flat on her back, laughing her head off, which probably set Sarah Ferguson-type alarm bells ringing at the palace.

William's own charity venture was a 1,000-mile bike trip across South Africa which he undertook with Harry. In all, 80 riders took part and the aim was to raise £250,000 for Unicef, the Nelson Mandela Children's Fund and Harry's charity Sentebale. In an eve-of-trip interview Harry said, "We never really spend any time together – we've got separate jobs going on at the moment.

"But it's great fun – well I don't know yet, we'll have to tell you. We might argue, we might have a bit of fun." Prince William joked, "The pain of spending a week with my brother is well worth it."

After the usual Christmas apart, William and Kate were reunited at Birkhall for a New Year holiday. By now Kate

PAGE 128: Looking the part, brothers William and Harry continue their military helicopter training at RAF Shawbury in June 2009.

PAGE 129: Deep in thought: William is surrounded by maps at his RAF Shawbury base but looks distracted, possibly with thoughts of an impending royal engagement.

OPPOSITE, LEFT: In another Issa gown, Kate attends a Starlight Children's Foundation party at the international renowned Saatchi Gallery in Chelsea, London in September 2009.

OPPOSITE, RIGHT: In an outfit that would surely impress Her Majesty, Kate attends the August 2009 wedding of Captain Nicholas Van Cutsem and Alice Hadden-Paton at The Guards Chapel. William also attended and was teasingly told, "You'll be next!"

ABOVE: Establishing himself as a working royal, Prince William bravely holds a giant tarantula spider at London's Natural History Museum. The prince was opening the second phase of the Darwin Centre, which houses the museum's 20 million insect and plant specimens.

was working for the family business, Party Pieces. She was reportedly training in website design and launching a new promotion called First Birthdays. It helped to offset some of the criticism that she wasn't the highest of achievers, career-wise, and more importantly it gave her time off whenever William was free to meet her.

William began his training at RAF Shawbury, in Shropshire, on 11 January 2009, two days after he enjoyed a birthday dinner and farewell party rolled into one at the Middletons' home.

The same month it was announced that William and Harry would be setting up their own offices in St James's Palace, headed by their private secretary, Jamie Lowther-Pinkerton, a former SAS officer, who had also been an equerry to the Queen Mother in the early 1980s.

In May, Harry also arrived at Shawbury where he started his training as an Army air helicopter pilot. The two brothers shared a rented cottage and tackled the usual domestic chores of cooking and ironing, as any other trainee would do.

In a joint interview they talked about the novelty of sharing a rented cottage and tackling housework – with William claiming he was the one in charge. "Bearing in mind I cook, I feed him [Harry] every day, I think he's done very well," he said.

"Harry does do washing up but then he leaves most of it in the sink and then I come back in the morning and I have to wash it up." William continued, "I do a fair bit of tidying up after him. He snores a lot, too. He keeps me up all night long."

At this point Harry pulled a face and joked, "Oh God, they'll think we share a bed now. We're brothers not lovers!" As Harry explained it would be the "first time, last time we'll live together", William added dryly, "It's been an emotional experience."

The sightings of William and Kate were getting fewer and fewer. In May 2009, they met up when William was on leave and attended a charity polo match at Coworth Park near Ascot. They had spent the previous night at his private apartment at Clarence House, where Kate had asked him to install a basic gym, so she could keep toned without having to go to a health club.

During the same leave, William made a private visit to meet

109-year-old Catherine Masters at the Grange Care Centre in Standford in the Vale, Oxfordshire. Earlier in the year, Mrs Masters had contacted Buckingham Palace to complain that her annual birthday card from the Queen was always the same design. Having accrued quite a stack of them over the years, she was tired of seeing Her Majesty in the same canary yellow dress. William apologized and promised to ensure his grandmother was wearing a different outfit next year.

Later in the summer, the prince was photographed kissing the other Catherine in his life, when he and Kate enjoyed a brief smooch in the car park of The Potting Shed, in the village

BELOW: The Princes visit the Mokolodi Nature Reserve in Botswana, Africa, in June 2010. Harry teases his older brother by pointing the head of a five-metre African Rock Python at him.

of Crudwell, a popular watering hole with the Cotswold polo playing set.

It was to stop such snatched photos appearing that prompted an authorized crackdown on the paparazzi in the run-up to the traditional Christmas break at Sandringham. A statement released on 5 December said that members of the royal family would now be prepared to take legal action against what they see as the "intrusive and unacceptable behaviour" of photographers.

The crackdown once again fuelled rumours that a royal engagement was in the offing, and once again the media crossed its collective fingers and waited in vain.

However, 2010 would finally provide the royal news that so many people had begun to suspect would never happen.

ABOVE: British Prime Minister David Cameron, retired Wing Commander Bob Foster and Prince William watch the flypast at the Battle of Britain Service of Thanksgiving and Rededication at Westminster Abbey in September 2010.

OPPOSITE: William and Harry visit the Semonkong Children's Centre in Lesotho. Following in their mother's footsteps, the princes are showing an increased interest in charity work.

8
ENGAGEMENT

" The Prince of Wales is delighted to announce the engagement of Prince William to Miss Catherine Middleton. The wedding will take place in the Spring or Summer of 2011, in London. Following the marriage, the couple will live in North Wales, where Prince William will continue to serve with the Royal Air Force "

Clarence House Statement, November 2010

LEFT: Although they actually got engaged in October 2010, Kate and Prince William chose 16 November to announce the news to the world. The 2011 wedding is set to be the largest royal event since the prince's parents, Prince Charles and Lady Diana, were married on 29 July 1981.

ABOVE: On the day the royal engagement was announced William's father, Prince Charles, was visiting his Poundbury model village in Dorset; Charles said he was "thrilled" at the news, adding, "it makes me feel very old!"

PREVIOUS PAGE: Royal grandeur: the world's press gather for a photocall in the State Rooms of St James's Palace as Prince William and Kate Middleton announce their engagement in November 2010

illiam and Kate spent Christmas 2009 apart, as royal partners only receive an invitation to join the festivities at Sandringham after they are engaged. Shortly before 11 o'clock on Christmas Day, William walked through the snow-laden paths of the Queen's Norfolk estate to attend matins at the tiny church of St Mary Magdalene. Kate meanwhile enjoyed a family Christmas with her parents, sister and brother in Bucklebury.

They met up for New Year at Birkhall and again two weeks later when William successfully completed his advanced helicopter-training course. He was presented with his certificate by his father at a ceremony at RAF Shawbury on 15 January. Kate was in the audience and rose to her feet and applauded enthusiastically when the prince's name was announced.

In the past, William has often looked tense when Kate is present, perhaps sensing that they are the focus of attention and a distraction, whether they are at a royal ceremony or attending a friend's wedding. Throughout 2010 they threw caution to the wind and appeared relaxed and happy on the few occasions they were seen together. At Shawbury for instance, Kate sat next to the prince throughout the ceremony, their body language less tense, as they smiled broadly and whispered to each other.

In his speech, Prince Charles spoke about the dangers facing a search and rescue pilot as well as poking fun at some of the less onerous tasks: "Some of you no doubt will find yourselves in Afghanistan where the ground troops will put great faith in you.

"Others no doubt among you will be plucking people from danger, maybe sheep in distress, not to mention endless ladies with conveniently sprained ankles on awkward mountainsides across the country."

Later in the month Flt Lt Wales arrived at RAF Anglesey to start his training, hoping to become a fully operational pilot by the summer, having learned the skills required to operate Sea King Helicopters.

Meanwhile, the prince also took another important step forward in his apprenticeship as monarch when he represented the Queen at the opening of the new £38-million Supreme Court in Wellington during a five-day visit to New Zealand. It was to be his first official overseas trip and he told officials

BELOW: News of the royal engagement sent the world's media into overdrive; this London news stand was hot off the press with the announcement.

it meant "an awful lot" to him. During his tour he showed he was imbued with the qualities of both his parents. His visit to the wildlife reserve of Kapiti Island off the north island's western coast, a haven for rare birds, mirrored the environmental concerns of his father. Earlier, his easy relationship with members of the public on a walkabout in Wellington evoked memories of Diana's people skills.

When Meryl Best, 41, told him she had been "privileged" to meet Diana on her visit to Christchurch in 1983, the prince asked: "What was she doing?" "She was looking beautiful," came the affectionate reply. William responded with "She did that elegantly", and then, after shaking more hands, he turned to Mrs Best a second time and said gratefully, "You are a very special lady. I will shake your hand again."

A month later, the prince charmed another crowd, this time a homegrown one, outside London's Royal Opera House, when he made his first appearance at the British Academy Film Awards. The 27-year-old royal received some of the loudest screams of the

A-list celebrity-packed night, with girls clamouring to kiss him and to be photographed with him.

Dressed in a dinner suit, the prince walked on stage with the Hollywood star Uma Thurman to present a BAFTA fellowship to legendary actress Vanessa Redgrave. Despite being an avowed republican, Ms Redgrave bowed down on bended knee and was beaming as William helped her back to her feet and kissed her on both cheeks.

In June, William and Harry travelled to Africa to carry out their first official joint overseas engagements when they visited Botswana, Lesotho and South Africa on behalf of three charities: Tusk Trust, Sentebale and the Football Association. Sentebale was jointly founded by Harry and Prince Seeiso of Lesotho and the latter joined the two brothers as they rode on horseback to visit schools and orphanages in the country's snow-capped

ABOVE: Kate's engagement ring is that worn by William's mother when she got engaged to Prince Charles. William said that giving Kate the ring – a dazzling oval blue 18-carat sapphire and diamond piece – was his way of ensuring that his late mother was involved in the occasion.

LEFT: In Bucklebury, Michael and Carole Middleton deliver a statement outside their home following the news of the engagement; the parents of the bride-to-be said they were "absolutely delighted" at the news.

OPPOSITE: After years of speculation about their future, William and Kate announced their engagement in November 2010. Asked why he had taken so many years to propose, the Prince said, "I didn't realize it was a race! But the time is right now, we're both very, very happy and I'm very glad that I have done it."

mountains. They wore grey knitted blankets like those worn by local Basotho herdsmen. The children had embroidered "Prince William Arthur Philip Louis" on his, while his brother's had the touching message, "Thank You Harry".

William's next visit to Africa was a Kenyan safari with Kate in October 2010 and, as we discovered in due course, it was to be a pretty unforgettable holiday since it was here that he proposed to the woman who had been by his friend and companion for eight years. Later William would only reveal the exact location was "somewhere nice in Kenya" – pretty much an understatement as it was in Mount Kenya National Park, at one of the lakes on the side of the mountain.

The prince hired a helicopter to take him and Kate to Lake Rutundu and Lake Alice, which are surrounded by snowy peaks and forests of heather. They flew from the Lewa Downs safari lodge in which he and Kate had stayed with Jecca Craig's family

ABOVE: The day after the royal engagement was announced, the British press made a big splash of the news across its front pages.

144

RIGHT: News of an impending royal wedding made headlines all around the world – these front pages are from Germany and Switzerland.

five years earlier. He had been carrying his mother's sapphire-and-diamond engagement ring in his rucksack and, in this most sublime of settings, produced it to an unsuspecting Kate and asked her to be his wife.

There are strong links between the royal family and Kenya. It was against this same backdrop that William's grandmother became Queen at the tender age of 25 when her father died suddenly in his sleep, while she and Prince Philip were on tour, staying at Treetops Hotel in Aberdare National Park.

William had spent part of his gap year working in North Kenya and later said, "It was the happiest time of my life," as none of his companions on anti-poaching patrols knew about his background and for once he enjoyed a rare period of anonymity.

Back home again, the question now was how to keep the news a secret until the official announcement. They had one joint public appearance to make on 24 October at the wedding of their friends Harry Meade and Rosie Bradford in Northleach, Gloucestershire.

It was the first time Kate had been seen since attending polo at the Beaufort Club on 10 July. She looked stunning in an electric blue silk dress with a black jacket and hat. In the past they have nearly always arrived separately to avoid being photographed together and so royal commentators interpreted the couple's arrival side by side as "very unusual and very

significant". "Will they be next?" queried one headline. Rumours abounded that they had already got engaged while on a trip to Balmoral, which Clarence House could legitimately dismiss as "categorically untrue".

The death of Kate's grandfather Peter Middleton on 2 November delayed the official announcement. Eventually it came on Tuesday 16 November, and although it had been anticipated for years, it seemed like a bolt out of the blue, as everyone had become accustomed to the status quo.

A statement from Clarence House proclaimed that the "Prince of Wales is delighted to announce the engagement of Prince William to Miss Catherine Middleton." In tune with the modern age, the news was posted on the Queen's Facebook page and as a "tweet" on the royal Twitter site, as well as by the old-fashioned e-mail method.

After a massive press call at St James's Palace at 4.45 pm, in which the couple posed amid a blitz of flashguns, they pre-recorded an interview with Tom Bradby, ITV's political editor, and former royal correspondent. William's press secretary, Miguel Head, in a press note to media organizations, said, "The couple asked to record this interview specifically with Mr Bradby, whom they have both known for some time."

ABOVE: Home sweet home for the newly married couple will be on Anglesey, on the north-west tip of Wales; Prince William is currently on a three-year posting as a Search and Rescue helicopter pilot based at RAF Valley, near Holyhead.

William admitted, "We had been talking about marriage for a while, so it wasn't a massively big surprise. I'd been planning it for a while, but as any guy out there will know, it takes a certain amount of motivation to get yourself going."

He revealed that he took so long to propose because he wanted Kate to have the chance to "back out" if she felt that she could not cope with life as a future queen.

Although everyone is familiar with Kate's features, few outside the magic royal circle had ever heard her speak and, given that she must have been nervous, Kate was surprisingly articulate, and spoke with a well-modulated tone. Recalling the proposal, she laughed as she said, "It was very romantic. There's a true romantic in there." She also revealed that the proposal had been as much of a surprise to her as it was to the rest of us, "Because we were out with friends and things, so I really didn't expect it all. I thought he might have maybe thought about it but no. It was a total shock when it came."

William talked candidly about his mother. Her sapphire-and-diamond ring "is very special to me," he said. "As Kate's very special to me now, it was right to put the two together." Referring poignantly to Diana, he added, "Because obviously she's not going to be around to share any of the fun and excitement of it all – this was my way of keeping her close to it all."

The prince was asked if he'd sought Michael Middleton's permission. "Well, I was torn between asking Kate's dad first and then the realization that he might actually say 'no' dawned upon

LEFT: RAF Valley – with its welcome sign in English and Welsh – is many miles away from London's boutiques and bars. However, the couple are said to relish the privacy afforded by rural North Wales.

me. So I thought if I ask Kate first then he can't really say no. So I did it that way round. I managed to speak to Mike soon after it happened really and then it sort of happened from there."

Kate added that her mother was "absolutely over the moon". She also said, "And actually we had quite an awkward situation because I knew that William had asked my father but I didn't know if my mother knew. So I came back from Scotland and my mother didn't make it clear to me whether she knew or not, so both of us were there sort of looking at each other and feeling quite awkward about it. But it was amazing to tell her and obviously she was very happy for us."

Referring to her family as "important to me", Kate added, "I hope we will be able to have a happy family ourselves," while William, joked, "I think we'll take it one step at a time. We'll sort of get over the marriage first and then maybe look at the kids. But obviously we want a family so we'll have to start thinking about that."

At one point Kate admitted, "It's obviously nerve-wracking, because I don't know the ropes really." William was more relaxed and jokey about the stress they'd been under: "We're like sort of ducks, very calm on the surface with little feet going under the water. It's been really exciting. We've been talking about it for a long time, so for us it's a real relief and it's really nice to be able to tell everybody."

News of the royal romance was immediately flashed around the world, with news stations such as ABC's *Good Morning America* opening with a trumpeted fanfare over photos of the couple. In Britain, Prime Minister David Cameron said the engagement marked "a great day for Britain". The Queen said she was "absolutely delighted" for them, while Prince Charles joked that "they have been practising long enough". Speaking from his Berkshire home, Michael Middleton said, "We have got to know William really well. We all think he is wonderful and we are extremely fond of him. They make a lovely couple."

Perhaps the most touching comment came from the man who for so long has been William's best friend, and will soon be Kate's brother-in-law, Prince Harry, who said, "I'm delighted that my brother has popped the question. It means I get a sister, which I have always wanted."

PAGE 148: The Middletons' home in Bucklebury was besieged with photographers as soon as the engagement was announced, and a police guard became the norm.

OPPOSITE: On their first public appearance together since announcing their engagement, William and Kate attended a Teenage Cancer Trust charity fundraising gala in Thursford, Norfolk in December 2010.

9

AN ABBEY WEDDING

"I'm sure the whole House will wish to join me in sending our warmest congratulations and best wishes to Prince William and Kate Middleton on their engagement. I'm sure everyone agrees this is wonderful news, we look forward to the wedding itself with excitement and anticipation."

Prime Minister David Cameron issues a statement in the House of Commons, November 2010

LEFT: Kate Middleton arrives at St Andrew's Church, Aldborough, Yorkshire, for the wedding of Harry Aubrey-Fletcher and Sarah Louise Stourton on 8 January 2011. Prince William, a longstanding friend of the groom, was also present – and no doubt he and Kate cast their minds forward to April and their own wedding ceremony.

The marriage of a monarch or a future monarch is a relatively rare occurrence in modern British history. There were four coronations during the whole of the 20th century but only three future monarchs were married in those same hundred years.

The Queen married Lt Philip Mountbatten at Westminster Abbey in 1947. Her father, later King George VI (the subject of the film *The King's Speech*), married Lady Elizabeth Bowes-Lyon at the Abbey in 1923, and of course Charles, Prince of Wales married Lady Diana Spencer in St Paul's Cathedral in 1981.

In organizing their 2011 wedding, Prince William and Kate Middleton needed to balance this historical continuity with their natural desire to have a very personal service surrounded

ABOVE: Lady Elizabeth Bowes-Lyon – the Queen's mother – leaves her home for her wedding to the Duke of York, the future King George VI, at Westminster Abbey on 26 April 1923.

LEFT: Westminster Abbey has long been a venue for royal weddings – the first, between King Henry I of England and Matilda of Scotland, took place in November 1100.

PREVIOUS PAGES: Sir George Hayter's painting captures the 1840 wedding of Queen Victoria and Prince Albert of Saxe-Coburg-Gotha. Victoria's wedding gown was a relatively simple affair – her dress was of white Spitalfields satin with a low neckline, fitted bodice and full-pleated skirt. Her gown was trimmed with bobbin Honiton lace and her face was concealed by a wedding veil, which she helped to popularize.

by friends and family. They also had to take into account the
public relations nightmare of holding a hugely expensive event
in the current economic climate while still offering the country
some of the much-loved pomp and circumstance that we
associate with a royal wedding.

by friends and family. They also had to take into account the
public relations nightmare of holding a hugely expensive event
in the current economic climate while still offering the country
some of the much-loved pomp and circumstance that we
associate with a royal wedding.

The choice of venue was relatively straightforward. Of
the three main contenders the first was St George's Chapel,
Windsor, which over a nine-year period hosted the wedding
of Prince Edward and Sophie Rhys Jones in 1999, the blessing
of Prince Charles's marriage to Camilla Parker Bowles and the
2008 wedding of William's cousin Peter Phillips to Autumn
Kelly. The main disadvantage here is that Windsor itself, with its
narrow streets and pavements, couldn't cope with the hundreds

*ABOVE: Princess Elizabeth is driven
along the Mall to Westminster Abbey
in the Irish State Coach with a
sovereign's escort of the Household
Cavalry for her marriage to Philip
Mountbatten on 20 November 1947*

*ABOVE: Crowds line the route as the
newly married Princess Elizabeth
and Prince Philip make their way
back to Buckingham Palace in a
glass coach drawn by white horses
after the service at Westminster
Abbey*

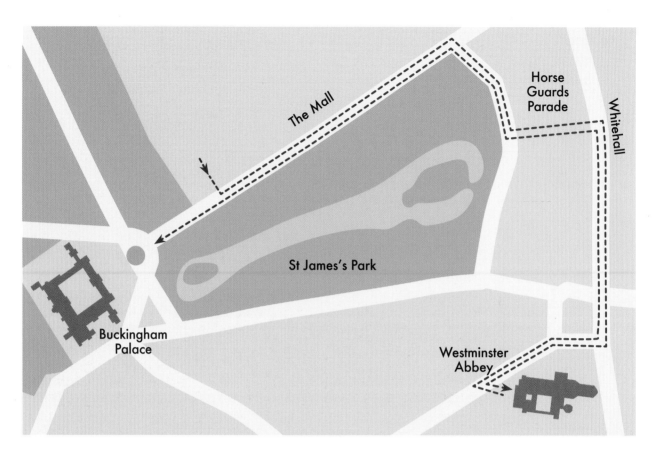

ABOVE: The wedding route – Kate will travel to Westminster Abbey by car via The Mall, Horse Guards Parade, Whitehall and Parliament Square. After the service, the newlyweds will return along the same route and travel in a carriage procession to Buckingham Palace.

of thousands who would descend on it to see the carriage procession after the service, and the route itself would be a relatively short one. Also, of course, the public would be denied the famous balcony appearance – with a likely kiss for the bride – which is possible only at Buckingham Palace.

The second choice was St Paul's Cathedral. This seemed an unlikely venue since for millions it will always be linked with the wedding of Charles and Diana, a union that Archbishop Runcie famously said was "the stuff of fairytales" but very soon turned into a living nightmare. Charles selected St Paul's mainly because he has always adored the building, once calling it "our greatest national monument". Also the marriage of the Prince of Wales was a State Occasion and representatives of all parts of the British establishment were invited together with overseas heads of state, ambassadors and so on, and the cathedral accommodates a far larger congregation than the Abbey.

St Paul's was soon crossed off the list by William and Kate. The processional routeway is three times longer than the one to the Abbey, making it prohibitively expensive to police. As heir

BELOW: Once Prince William and Kate Middleton are married in Westminster Abbey on 29 April they and their families will return to Buckingham Palace in a procession of horse-drawn carriages via Horse Guards Parade, site of the annual Trooping the Colour ceremonies.

to the heir, William didn't feel that he needed such a lavish array of official guests, many of whom he would never have met in his life. His and Kate's ideal was always to try to make the service as personal as possible. Over the past five years the couple have been guests at more than a dozen weddings, nearly all of them in traditional rural churches, and one of their aims has been to replicate the intimate feeling of having friends and family together in a fabulous setting that doesn't overwhelm in the way that St Paul's can.

The Abbey seemed a natural choice. It has strong links with the monarchy. For instance, like St George's Chapel, it is a royal peculiar, as it comes directly under the jurisdiction of the

ABOVE: Princess Elizabeth and Prince Philip kneel at the High Altar in front of the Archbishop of Canterbury during their marriage ceremony in Westminster Abbey in 1947, flanked by their respective families. The Queen and Prince Philip will sit to the right in April 2011 when William and Kate take centre stage.

Queen rather than a diocese. This was an extremely important privilege in the Middle Ages as it gave the Abbey full control over its finances and it soon became one of the wealthiest churches in the country.

Another appeal for the young couple is the layout of the Abbey which is almost like a church within a church. The wedding service will take place watched by close friends in the Quire area and with the couple and their families slightly to the east in the Sacrarium. All of these people will have an unimpeded view of proceedings, and the couple themselves will feel they have a certain amount of privacy, as most of the congregation will be in the nave and the two transepts, which are outside this area.

Another bonus for William is that a royal insider, Sir Stephen Lamport, who was Charles's private secretary until 2002, is now Receiver General of the Abbey and responsible for organizing major events there.

Given that finance is an overriding issue with this wedding, it helps that the route to and from the Abbey goes mostly past royal and government buildings in The Mall, Whitehall and Parliament Square, making it easier to police than if it covered business and residential areas.

The processional routeway is one of the reasons the Abbey was turned into a popular venue for royal weddings. In the nineteenth and earlier centuries the procession wasn't a key element of the day and also the marriage services themselves were nearly always held in private, smaller venues. When Queen Victoria married Prince Albert in February 1840 she opted for the Chapel Royal. After the ceremony, the myrtle from her bouquet was planted, and every royal bride since has had a sprig from it woven into her own bouquet.

The Queen's eldest daughter, Victoria, the Princess Royal, married Prince Frederick of Prussia at the same venue, and they were to become the parents of Germany's Emperor William II – "Kaiser Bill". In 1893, the future George V and Queen Mary – the grandparents of Queen Elizabeth II – were also married here.

For William, the Chapel Royal has sad memories because it is here that his mother's body lay after its return to Britain following her fatal car crash, and it was here that he and Harry paid their private respects on the night before her funeral.

ABOVE: *Prince William and Kate Middleton will be married by the Archbishop of Canterbury, Rowan Williams (right), seen here with the Very Reverend John Hall, Dean of Westminster, who will conduct the service.*

At the beginning of the twentieth century, The Mall was created as a ceremonial routeway to match similar ones in Paris, Berlin, Washington and Rome. At the same time, the main façade of Buckingham Palace, on the east side, was redesigned using Portland stone and the Queen Victoria Memorial was built and unveiled in 1911.

The Mall was intended to be used for major national ceremonies and also to link it to the Abbey which now began to be used for royal weddings for the first time since medieval days. In 1919, Princess Patricia of Connaught – a granddaughter of Queen Victoria, and popularly known as "Princess Pat" – married Captain Alexander Ramsay. Like William, she was marrying outside the blood royal, and was happy to forfeit her royal title to do so. Henceforth she was known as Lady Patricia Ramsay.

The First World War had only been over three months, so, as with William and Kate's wedding, it was decided to cut back on cost and declare it a "khaki wedding" with all the men in uniform.

ABOVE: On a previous visit to Westminster Abbey for a royal wedding Prince William was a pageboy for Prince Andrew and Sarah Ferguson in July 1986. Aged four and dressed in a sailor outfit and boater hat, William's attention often wandered from the main event!

In 1923 Albert, Duke of York, the second son of King George V, married Lady Elizabeth Bowes-Lyon. Although she was the daughter of an earl, it is unlikely that he would have been encouraged to marry her had he been Prince of Wales and heir. Royalty was expected to marry royalty, although the abolition of monarchies in Russia, Germany, Austria and Turkey after the First World War didn't leave much to choose from. Ironically, the future Queen Mother – commoner or not – became one of the best loved royal figures of recent times.

Once again, costs were a factor and the king refused to allow stands to be built in the Abbey to accommodate extra guests, so 1,780 people were invited instead of a possible 2,600. On her way to the altar, Elizabeth spontaneously knelt and placed her bouquet on the Tomb of the Unknown Soldier, perhaps a mark of respect for her brother Fergus who was killed at the Battle of Loos in 1915.

An expected worldwide audience of one billion will watch some or all of William and Kate's wedding. But, in 1923, the Archbishop of Canterbury vetoed the idea of a live broadcast on the wireless in case it was heard in public houses where the audience of men might not remove their hats!

The wedding of 21-year-old Princess Elizabeth on 20 November 1947 was just over two years after the Second World War finally ended with victory over Japan. Britain was in dire straits economically. Food shortages meant people were rationed to 1 oz of bacon a week and 2 oz of butter, and George VI was concerned that the wedding should not generate an extra burden for the country. Fortunately, 26-year-old Philip Mountbatten was happy to go along with this. On the day of his engagement he arrived at Buckingham Palace in naval uniform. A lady in waiting later recalled, "I noticed that his uniform was shabby – it had the usual after-the-war look – and I liked him for not having got a new one for the occasion, as many men would have done to make an impression."

The Labour government gave Princess Elizabeth 200 extra clothing coupons towards her trousseau and well-meaning women, caught up in the romance, sent in their own coupons, all of which had to be returned as it was illegal to give coupons away. The Household Cavalry escorted the bride's

ABOVE: During the 1986 wedding of Prince Andrew and Sarah Ferguson, when Prince William wasn't clowning with bridesmaid Laura Fellowes – at one point he even sticks out his tongue – he was playing with his hat.

procession, the first time the soldiers had appeared in plumes and breastplates since the before the war. Little wonder Winston Churchill called the wedding "a flash of colour on the hard road we have to travel". Again it was a khaki wedding with men in uniform. Royal ladies – there were seven queens present as well as six kings – wore their finest jewels, although as Princess Juliana of the Netherlands noted sniffily few had bothered to have them cleaned.

At the palace, 150 guests enjoyed an "austerity" wedding breakfast – the regal name for a reception. One of the problems of a royal wedding in London is that only a fraction of the guests present at the Abbey can be seated for a meal at Buckingham

ABOVE: A worldwide TV audience of 500 million tuned in as Prince Andrew wed Sarah Ferguson on 23 July 1986. The glorious setting of Westminster Abbey can be seen in full as Prince Andrew and his new bride make their way down the nave to the main door of the Abbey.

RIGHT: When 21-year-old Princess Elizabeth married Prince Philip, five years her senior, the bride wore a sumptuous ivory silk bridal gown and a 13-ft star-patterned circular train designed by Norman Hartnell; the groom was in naval uniform.

ABOVE: The marriage of Prince Edward and Sophie Rhys-Jones on 19 June 1999 took place not at Westminster Abbey but at St George's Chapel at Windsor Castle. Following the marriage, Sophie became Her Royal Highness The Countess of Wessex.

Palace. To get round this William and Kate have opted for a buffet reception immediately after the wedding with a more select number invited to a dinner-dance later in the day.

Princess Anne was always better known for her interest in horses than fashion. The down to earth, hard-working, no-nonsense royal wasn't cast in the fairytale princess mould. Nevertheless, on her wedding day, 14 November 1973, which was also her brother Charles's 25th birthday, she looked stunning in the Tudor-style gown designed by Maureen Small.

Anne's "something borrowed" was a diamond fringe tiara belonging to the Queen Mother, who had also loaned it to the Queen for her 1947 wedding. The princess had been a bridesmaid many times and in her own words had to manage "yards of uncontrollable children", so at her own wedding she had only two attendants: her cousin Lady Sarah Armstong Jones as bridesmaid and her brother Prince Edward as pageboy.

Diana Spencer, then aged 20, had to exchange her vows in front of a congregation of 3,000 and a television audience of 750 million. By 29 April 2011, Kate must hoping that nerves don't get the better of her, as they did Diana who mixed up the prince's names during the exchange of vows – calling him Philip Charles Arthur George. When the film was played for the royal family at a party at the Ritz later on, Prince Andrew called out, "She's married my father!"

Prince Charles, 32, in the full dress uniform of a naval commander, slightly muddled his vows, too, referring to "thy goods" rather than "my worldly goods". Many felt he had done it to make Diana feel more relaxed.

The last royal wedding at Westminster Abbey was that of Prince Andrew to Sarah Ferguson in July 1986. There were no wedding jitters for the uber-buoyant "Fergie" who said the night before: "I think it's going to be so exciting… It's going to

ABOVE: Sarah Ferguson looks radiant in her ivory duchesse satin dress alongside Prince Andrew, distinguished in his naval uniform, as the pair walk down the aisle in July 1986; however, the marriage lasted only ten years.

be the best day of my life – that's all there is about it." Among their many attendants was four-year-old Prince William, who entertained himself through the hour-long service by playing with the band on his hat and by sticking his tongue out at the bridesmaids.

Now, after the services at St George's Chapel for Prince Edward, Prince Charles, Peter Phillips and their brides, William and Kate have returned to Westminster Abbey which has witnessed 38 coronations, as well as the weddings of so many royal relations. In doing so, they have reinforced the links between the Abbey and monarchy that go back almost 950 years, and ensured that London – and more importantly themselves – has a day to remember.

ABOVE: Casting aside royal protocol and to the great delight of the cheering crowd, Prince William's parents Charles and Diana kiss on the balcony of Buckingham Palace following their wedding on 29 July 1981.

RIGHT: The impressive wedding cake made for Prince Charles and Lady Diana was prepared by Chief Petty Officer David Avery, an instructor at the Royal Naval Cookery School in Kent. The five-tiered fruitcake with icing and marzipan was adorned with emblems from the groom's naval days.

10
THE FUTURE

"Remember that you're marrying a beautiful man you are in love with and remember to make time for him – because I didn't. Andrew and I spent 40 days together in the first five years of our marriage."

Sarah Ferguson offers Kate some advice

LEFT: Sporting her engagement ring, Kate joins William for their first joint engagement since they revealed their wedding plans in November 2010. The couple arrived in Thursford, Norfolk, for a Christmas Spectacular in aid of the Teenage Cancer Trust. Kate wowed the crowd in a stunning black-and-white dress and fitted black jacket, complemented by a matching black handbag. The royal couple can expect a whole host of such occasions in the years to come.

ABOVE: The now-defunct Woolworths chain speculated in 2006 over the date of the royal engagement and showed their designs for a series of souvenirs including a plate. They left a space for the date, and were said to have even designed William and Kate pick-and-mix sweets.

By the time the bells of Westminster Abbey stop ringing and the crowds in The Mall take their banners and balloons home, the life of Catherine Middleton will have changed for ever. She will automatically have become an HRH, the third lady in the land, and every year the Union Flag will fly from all UK government buildings to mark her birthday. At the same time, she and Prince William will be spearheading a new type of royal marriage, one that's more attuned to modern times.

William and Kate's style of monarchy will reflect the legacy of both his parents. From his father he has inherited a belief in duty. In an interview at St Andrews, he said, "The monarchy is something that needs to be there – I just feel it's very, very important – it's a form of stability and I hope to be able to continue that." From his mother he is aware of the value of a more compassionate and less remote style which Kate has also studied closely, saying of Diana "I would have loved to have met her – she's an inspirational woman to look up to".

Marriage will bring some of the inevitable trappings of monarchy for Kate. William is likely to be offered a dukedom by the Queen and his new wife could be Duchess of Cambridge, Sussex, Clarence or one of the other available titles. She will also have her own coat of arms and a royal standard similar to the Queen's but with a white ermine-patterned design around it. She and William will also have their own joint cipher – a combination of their two initials. Normally these are interwoven, but having W.C. on top of the notepaper wouldn't look too good, so Kate's initial is likely to be above her husband's.

Kate will also accompany William to some of some of the key events in the royal calendar, from Trooping the Colour in June to the wreath laying at the Cenotaph on Remembrance Sunday. William has vowed to guide both Kate and, to a lesser extent, her family through the minefield of royal protocol and public duty. "I want to make sure they have the best guidance and the chance to see what life is like in the family." Speaking about his bride-to-be, William added, "I just wanted to give her the best chance to settle in." He has also asked his aunt, Prince Edward's wife, Sophie Wessex, to mentor Kate. Both women come from similar middle-class backgrounds and Sophie has successfully managed to balance her life as a working royal

ABOVE: Official Prince William and Kate Middleton Royal Wedding Commemorative china, "approved by HRH Prince William of Wales and Miss Catherine Middleton". The collection includes a tankard, plate and pillbox.

with her role as a mother to two young children.

Despite their respect for tradition, William and Kate are keen to bring some less formal touches to royal life. This became apparent when it was announced that Kate would arrive at Westminster Abbey by car rather than carriage. An aide explained, "Catherine chose to go by car because she wants a more low-key arrival, while she's still Miss Middleton at that point." Afterwards, the royals and their guests will enjoy a buffet rather than a banquet, followed later on by a dinner hosted by Prince Charles and then a dance.

While 20-year-old Diana was immediately thrown into

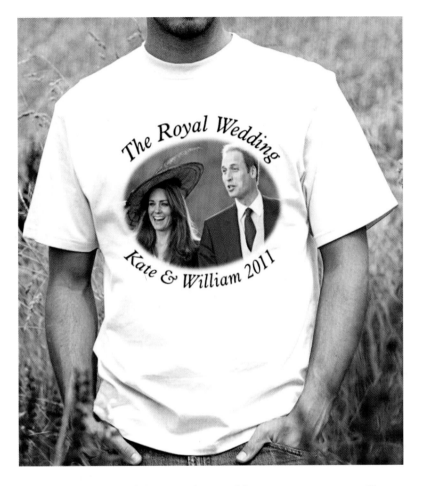

RIGHT: Barely had the headline appeared on the news when the Kate and William souvenir industry leaped into life. E-bay was one site where many people started selling merchandise, such as this T-shirt.

OPPOSITE: Formerly the home of the Queen Mother from 1953 to 2002, Clarence House is currently the official residence of the Prince of Wales and the Duchess of Cornwall, and Princes William and Harry.

PREVIOUS PAGES: The royal family take their places on the Buckingham Palace balcony for the 2010 Trooping the Colour pageant. Seen here are Princess Beatrice, Prince William, Prince Edward, Sophie, Countess of Wessex, the Queen, Prince and Princess Michael of Kent, Prince Philip, the Duchess of Cornwall and Prince Charles. From 2011, a new face – Kate – should join her husband for the event.

full-scale royal life following her wedding in 1981, Kate will take a different route. "I'm trying to learn from lessons done in the past," said William on the day of his engagement. To stop a repetition of the wave of adulation and press interest that threatened to engulf his young mother, William and Kate will retire to Anglesey as soon as the wedding fever has died down and Kate, for the most part, will take on the role of an officer's wife while William continues as a Search and Rescue pilot until the spring of 2013.

The retreat to North Wales has the full blessing of the Queen who fondly recalls the brief but happy spell she spent in Malta in the late 1940s when Prince Philip was stationed there during his navy days. For the only time in her life, the young Princess Elizabeth led a relatively normal life, having her hair done alongside other women in the local salon, hosting parties for other navy wives, and dining in local cafés with her new husband.

RIGHT: Kate should revel on the international scene alongside other glamorous consorts, such as Queen Rania of Jordan. A respected international philanthropist and known for her exceptional style, she is also a modern-day royal, boasting her own YouTube channel and Twitter account.

ABOVE: The first ever royal engagement coin – the Royal Mint coin has a value of £5 and has been approved by the Queen and Prince William.

Both Kate and William are happy to leave their nightclubbing times behind them. Life in rural North Wales is a remote whitewashed farmhouse, with its own beach and a short drive from the one of their favourite haunts, a pub they often slip away to for a cosy drink, the award-winning White Eagle in Rhoscolyn on the north-west coast of Anglesey. Bar staff say, "They're just like any other young couple in love – until you realize they've got armed bodyguards on the next table. Prince William usually drinks bitter, perhaps a pint or two, and Kate sticks to white wine and sparkling water."

William apparently enjoys the White Eagle's homemade burgers and chips. Kate, meantime, prefers fish and salads.

So far, the princess-in-waiting has been able to shop without being bothered by anyone at a nearby Tesco store, before cooking meals for William as well as hosting dinner parties for friends. William pays £750 a month for renting the farmhouse and there are currently no plans to move. The pair also regularly escape to Scotland, spending time at Birkhall, Charles's home on the Balmoral estate, and it wouldn't be surprising if they spent at least some of their honeymoon there.

After William leaves Search and Rescue in 2013 the couple are likely to move into a six-bedroomed house his father has had built at Harewood Park in Herefordshire. As you would expect from someone with Charles's passion for environment, it will be the most eco-friendly royal home to date with a reed-bed sewerage system, wood-chip boiler, solar panels and walls lined with insulating sheep's wool.

When in London they will have the use of William's apartment at Clarence House, and it is here that they will base themselves when they undertake engagements in the capital. William is involved with several charities and organizations. For example, in 2005 he became Patron of the Tusk Trust, a conservation charity of the type his father would be involved in, which aims to secure a peaceful co-existence for Africa's wildlife and its people. He is also involved with charities that Diana supported, such as Centrepoint, the UK's leading homeless charity, which William also joined in 2005; to prove he's not just a figurehead, the prince slept rough on the streets just before Christmas 2009 to highlight the issues faced by young homeless people.

RIGHT: Crown Princess Mary and Crown Prince Frederik of Denmark leave hospital with their newborn twins in January 2011 – the princess has often been compared to Princess Diana and Jacqueline Kennedy Onassis and has been named as one of the world's most fashionable women.

ABOVE: Kate Middleton will, in time, become the sixth Queen Catherine in British history. The first, Catherine of Valois (1401–37), married King Henry V and was crowned in 1421. After the King's death, Catherine had five children with Owen Tudor.

*ABOVE: Catherine of Aragon (1485–1536) was the first wife
of King Henry VIII. The Pope's refusal to let the King divorce
her led to the creation of the Church of England.*

RIGHT: Catherine Parr (1512–48) was the sixth and final wife of King Henry VIII and outlived him, she was the most married Queen of England, with four husbands during her lifetime.

RIGHT: Catherine Parr (1512–48) was the sixth and final wife of King Henry VIII and outlived him, she was the most married Queen of England, with four husbands during her lifetime.

LEFT: Catherine Howard (c.1520–42) was the fifth wife of King Henry VIII; the luckless Catherine was beheaded only a couple of years after their marriage.

Kate will bring youthful glamour to the Windsor brand and when she appears on the international scene will easily rival other beautiful consorts such as Queen Rania of Jordan and Crown Princess Mary of Denmark. At home being a great beauty and style icon will be an advantage, but the public also traditionally admires hardworking royals – the Queen, with her unflagging commitment to duty despite being in her mid-80s, and the workaholic Princess Royal are always singled out for praise in opinion polls.

Kate and her advisers will have to give some thought as to

LEFT: Catherine of Braganza (1638–1705); Queen to Charles II, she was unpopular due to her Catholic faith and her limited English.

what her role will be after William ends his RAF career in two years' time, and the couple take on more duties, and decide whether she will stay largely in the background or else become a major crusading figure on the world's stage as Diana became.

To make sure that Kate doesn't suffer the same level of press intrusion as his mother did, William has made it clear that he will enforce a "zero tolerance" stance to crack down on the paparazzi. He has instructed Gerrard Tyrrell, one of Britain's leading privacy lawyers, to consider either criminal or civil action against any photographer who oversteps the mark. He is said to have promised this to his fiancée's father, Michael Middleton, when he asked for his daughter's hand in marriage. He has also studied the landmark ruling from the European Court of Human Rights in 2004 won by Princess Caroline

RIGHT: An all too familiar situation for William as Kate is hounded by the paparazzi in similar circumstances to the photo above in which the prince's mother, Princess Diana, is seen trying to avoid the attentions of the press.

ABOVE: Ladies in red – an almost spooky comparison between Diana and Kate, both style icons of their day, as they wear very similar attire.

LEFT: Fashion queens – in an almost identical outfit, Kate suggests that she not only admires William, but his late mother, Diana, too.

of Monaco that prevented the German press from publishing photos of her and her children following years of harassment.

It could be several decades before the couple become monarch and consort. If the Queen lives to her mother's age, William could be in his mid-40s before he is even Prince of Wales and it might be another 20 years before he becomes King William V. Kate will become Queen Catherine, the sixth in British history, and the first consort to have been born with no aristocratic or royal title since Catherine Parr – the sixth and final wife of Henry VIII.

For Kate, the coming years will be full of challenges. She admitted at the time of her engagement, "It's nerve-wracking, because I don't know the ropes really," but thanks to the support network from both families, royal aides and advisers – and of course from William himself – she will have the best possible start to life as a princess.

Bibliography

Allison, Ronald, *The Royal Encyclopaedia*, Macmillan, London, 1991

Bradford, Sarah, *Elizabeth: A Biography of Her Majesty the Queen*, Heinemann, London, 1996

Dimbleby, Jonathan, *The Prince of Wales – A Biography*, Little Brown, London, 1994

Jobson, Robert, *William and Kate – The Love Story*, John Blake Publishing, London, 2010

Joseph, Claudia, *Kate: the Making of a Princess*, Mainstream, Edinburgh, 2010

Lloyd, Ian, *William: The People's Prince*, Pavilion, London, 2003

Morton, Andrew, *Diana: Her True Story in Her Own Words*, Michael O'Mara, London, 1997

Nicholl, Katie, *William and Harry*, Preface Publishing, London, 2010

Shawcross, William, *Queen Elizabeth the Queen Mother*, Macmillan, London, 2009

Credits

Author's Biography

Ian Lloyd has a degree in Medieval and Modern History from the University of Nottingham, as well as diplomas in photography, management and bookselling. He has been a professional writer and photographer for over 20 years and had produced articles for many UK magazines and newspapers including *Hello*, *Saga*, *Majesty*, *Radio Times*, *Classic FM Magazine*, the *Daily Mail*, the *Daily Telegraph* and the *Sunday Post*. He is the author of *Crown Jewel – A Year in the Life of the Queen Mother* (1989) and *William – The People's Prince* (2003).

As a royal commentator he appears frequently on Sky News, BBC News 24, BBC Breakfast, NBC, Fox News, Radio 5 Live, Radio Ulster and Radio Wales, and is also an after dinner speaker. He lives in Oxford.

www.ianlloyd.co.uk

Acknowledgements

The Publishers would like to thank Julie Etchingham, Michael Jermey and Mike Blair at ITV News for their help in the production of this book and also Kevin Morgan at ITV.

Picture Credits

The publishers would like to thank the following sources for their kind permission to reproduce the pictures in this book.

Key: t=Top, b=Bottom, c=Centre, l=Left and r=Right

Alamy: /StockImages: 50-51

The Bridgeman Art Library: /National Portrait Gallery, London, UK/Roger-Viollet, Paris/Portrait of Catherine Parr (1512-48) sixth wife of Henry VIII (1491-1547) (panel), English School, (16th century): 185, /Philip Mould Ltd, London/Private Collection, Portrait of a Lady, thought to be Catherine Howard (oil on panel), Holbein the Younger, Hans (1497/8-1543) (follower of): 184, /Philip Mould Ltd, London/Private Collection, Portrait of Catherine of Braganza (1638-1705), c.1665 (oil on canvas), Lely, Sir Peter (1618-80) (studio of): 186, /The Royal Collection © 2011 Her Majesty Queen Elizabeth II/The Marriage of Queen Victoria, on the 10th February 1840, 1840-42 (oil on canvas), Hayter, Sir George (1792-1871): 154-155

Corbis: /Atlantide Phototravel: 156, /Rune Hellestad: 178

DC Thomson: /Photographs © D.C.Thomson&Co.,Ltd Dundee www.dcthomson.co.uk: 60t, 60b, 61t, 61b

Getty: 81, 143t, 143b, 144, 174, /AFP: 23, /Scott Barbour: 117, / Tim Graham: 26, 90, 168, 170, 189, /Hulton Archive: 20, 147, 158, 159, 162, 183, /Mike Lusmore: 110, /Popperfoto: 167, 182, / Oli Scarff: 141, /WireImage: 136

Stephen Gibson: 64

Press Association Images: AJ/BB/UK Press: 44, 63, /David Cheskin/PA Archive: 46, /Mark Cuthbert/UK Press: 65, 77, 103, 150, /Anwar Hussein/Empics Entertainment: 58, /Antony Jones/ UK Press: 98, 106, /Pa Archive: 12, /Julian Parker/UK Press: 21, / John Stillwell/PA Archive: 62, 100, 142

Rex Features: 1, 4, 6, 8, 17, 18, 19, 24, 25t, 25b, 31, 40, 43, 52, 53, 59, 66, 68, 69, 70, 71, 72, 74, 76, 80, 86, 87,91, 93, 94, 95, 97, 99, 107, 114, 115, 121, 122, 132, 145, 163, 166, 129, 187, 188, /Nicholas Bailey: 161, /Malcolm Clarke/Associated Newspapers: 54, /Malcolm Clarke/Daily Mail: 55, /David Crump/ Daily Mail: 27, /Alan Davidson: 130l, /Michael Dunlea: 92, 108-109, 124, /Everett Collection: 16, /Richard Francis: 171, / James Fraser: 48, 49, 57, /Richard Gardner: 180t, /Paul Grover: 125, /David Hartley: 22, 88, 111, 148-149, /David Hartley/ Rupert Hartley: 128, 135, /Ikon Pictures Ltd: 112, 116, 130r, / Ikon Pictures/Niraj Tanna: 152, /Susannah Ireland: 138-139, /Nils Jorgensen: 169, /Jorgensen/Carraro/Young: 13, /Tony Kyriacou: 78, /Mark Large: 85, /Stephen Lock: 56, 82, 84, /Geoff Moore: 140, /Heathcliff O'Malley: 176-177, /Davidson/O'Neill: 126, / Harry Page: 24, /Matt Phelvin: 120, /Andrew Price: 146, /Tim Rooke: 10, 28, 75, 96, 101, 102, 104, 118, 127, 129, 133, 134, 172, 181, 190, /Royal Collection © 2010 HM Queen Elizabeth II: 175, /Royal Mint: 180b, /Jeremy Selwyn/Evening Standard: 79, / Geoffrey Swaine: 30, /Ray Tang: 45, /Today: 164l, 164r, 165, / Anthony Upton: 147, /Richard Young: 89

Solo Syndication: 34, 35, 36, 37, 38-39

Every effort has been made to acknowledge correctly and contact the source and/or copyright holder of each picture and Carlton Books Limited apologises for any unintentional errors or omissions, which will be, corrected in future editions of this book.

Publishers' Credits

Editorial Manager: Vanessa Daubney
Editor: David Lloyd
Additional editorial work: Victoria Marshallsay and Alice Payne
Art Director: Lucy Coley
Designer: Anna Pow
Picture Research: Jenny Meredith
Production Controller: Maria Petalidou